The Politics of
Revenue Sharing

The Politics of

Revenue Sharing

PAUL R. DOMMEL

INDIANA UNIVERSITY PRESS
Bloomington & London

Published in Canada by Fitzhenry & Whiteside Limited,
Don Mills, Ontario

Manufactured in the United States of America

Library of Congress Cataloging in Publication Data

    Dommel, Paul R.   1933-
      The politics of revenue sharing.

      Bibliography
      1. Intergovernmental fiscal relations—United
States. 2. Grants-in-aid—United States. 3. United
States—Politics and government—1969. I. Title.
HJ275.D65   336.1'85'0973 74-376
ISBN 0-253-34551-0

To Frances, Robyn,
David and Paul A.

Contents

Contents

Preface

In the pages that follow I have four major purposes: to set forth the political and legislative history of revenue sharing; to provide capsulized overviews of the public policy process in the United States; to raise some normative questions about revenue sharing and suggest some criteria by which the policy can be evaluated; to do all of these as concisely and as conversationally as possible. Writing about a policy area that is continuing to evolve is something of a risky business in that one cannot comfortably take cosmic views, and, at the same time, the writer must avoid being beguiled by every new headline in the newspaper. I hope that between these two extremes, I can say something of use and meaning about the politics of revenue sharing.

The material for this volume was obtained from a variety of sources, including government documents, newspaper articles, general literature, a Congressional survey, and correspondence and interviews with about twenty-five persons involved in one way or another with development and implementation of revenue sharing policy. I wish to acknowledge the special help of Mike Bird, Staff Economist of the Joint Congressional Committee on Internal Revenue Taxation, and Murry Weidenbaum, Professor of Economics at Washington University and former Assistant Secretary of the Treasury, who kindly read and commented on portions of the manuscript. My appreciation also to Professor Samuel Beer of Harvard for his valued comments and suggestions. I would also like to acknowledge the help of the Research and Publications Committee of Holy Cross College which provided the financial assistance to make this research possible. To this list I would also add Pearl Jolicoeur, my speedy and accurate typist.

P.R.D.

The Politics of
Revenue Sharing

Introduction

1971—". . .we are for revenue sharing, and we are for it strongly. I am not going to repeat over and over again that we are for sharing. It goes without saying that we are strongly for it, and each one of us will tell you why."

> Mayor John V. Lindsay, Chairman, Legislative Action Committee, U.S. Conference of Mayors, testifying before the House Ways and Means Committee, June 11, 1971

1972—"This program will mean both a new source of revenue for State and local governments and a new sense of responsibility.

"We expect great things from this program—and we are going to be watching for them."

> President Nixon, statement issued at signing of revenue sharing law, Philadelphia, Pa., Oct. 20, 1972

1973—". . .general revenue sharing has not turned out to be the savior we had hoped for.

"The New Federalism has turned out to be a Trojan horse for American cities. A gift left behind by an administration retreating from its basic responsibilities to the citizens."

> Mayor Wes Uhlman of Seattle, Wash., statement submitted to the Senate Subcommittee on Intergovernmental Relations, Feb. 21, 1973

In less than two years revenue sharing had been transformed in the minds of some city mayors from a program of salvation to what Mayor Henry W. Maier of Milwaukee termed a "cruel hoax" and a "gigantic double-cross." Why this change of opinion? Was there a "double-cross?" If so, should the mayors have been so shocked and surprised in early 1973 as they seemingly were? What troubled them was that revenue sharing, which had been presented by the Nixon administration in 1971 as a program of "add on" money, was being used in 1973 as a means of liquidating a large number of other grant programs and thus was going to the states and communities as "substitute" money.

It is the contention of this book that there was an inevitability about this turn of events. The mayors, with closer study, perhaps would not have been so eager to switch from opposition to revenue sharing in the mid-1960's to being leading proponents of the plan in the late 1960's. What the mayors either did not know, or chose to overlook, was that while they, along with governors, state legislators, county officials, and city managers, were interested in the money, there were others interested in getting the federal government out of the grant-in-aid business. The mayors, governors, and their allies were properly concerned about the fiscal potential of revenue sharing as a means of dealing with growing budgetary and taxation problems at the state and local levels of government. But in this concern, they ignored the political history of the issue, a history clearly showing that the early support for the plan came from those persons in Congress with a record of both opposing grant-in-aid programs and offering revenue sharing as a substitute for such grants. Also, what the mayors apparently did not know was that while President Nixon and top officials of his administration were presenting tax sharing as additional money, the President himself continued to be interested in tax sharing as a means of cashing in all federal grants.

It is the purpose of this book to examine this political history of tax sharing. The study will be done within the broader context of public policy making, which will focus on the political interplay between the Congress, the President, and interest groups, as revenue sharing moved from a little known concept of intergovernmental fiscal relations to a highly visible and controversial policy innovation. This requires an historical sketch of how the federal aid system evolved; why discontent with this aid developed; how revenue sharing appeared as a proposed remedy; who favored it, who opposed it, and why. How was the coalition (of which the mayors became a major partner) built to get the bill passed in Congress, where it had been pigeonholed for more than five years? What happened to bring on the disillusionment?

As public policy is formulated, legitimated, and applied, it must clear a series of strategic points at which proponents and opponents do battle. Control of these points is critical for both sides and it is a necessary part of any policy study to determine the critical points on a particular issue and to examine the nature of the politics at these points. Each policy issue has its own political scenario as it moves from formulation to implementation, but each issue is also influenced and molded by the interactions of the institutions themselves. The President and Congress compete for power and major issues get caught up in this competition. Revenue sharing plays a central role in the test of strength between President Nixon and the Democratic-controlled Congress. Within these institutions there are rules of the game that further influence the policy process. All of these factors are essential not only to understanding the politics of revenue sharing, but also to grasping the nature of the policy process of the American political system. The politics of revenue sharing presents a model case of the politics of public policy making.

This, however, is not the only perspective from which the politics of revenue sharing must be examined. The question of the effectiveness of tax sharing in solving urban problems cannot be clearly answered. The contention is that providing funds to state and local governments through revenue sharing with no strings attached to the use of the money will prove a more effective fiscal transfer device for problem solving than the predominant categorical grant approach that earmarks funds to narrow, specific purposes. The argument outwardly is simple: state and local governments are closer to the problems and therefore understand them better than the distant Washington bureaucracy. To state that the existing system has not solved our problems does not, however, provide the evidence that tax sharing will. There is no objective evidence to show that revenue sharing will improve the quality of education or life in our cities any more than the existing forms of aid. At this stage, one is forced to rely on the persuasiveness of the arguments that have been made and on one's own judgment.

Formation of judgments can be aided, however, by considering another dimension of politics. Politics in this sense does not refer to partisan politics, but rather to the consequences of tax sharing in terms of the allocation of public resources. Decisions on public spending are highly political since there is not enough money available to do everything everyone wants done. As a result, decision makers must assign priorities. A major historical purpose of the federal grant-in-aid system has been to assign national priorities in some areas by stating the purpose for which money is to be spent and overseeing the expenditures to assure that these purposes are adhered to. Revenue sharing transfers a portion of this priority-setting assignment to state and local officials who will select the purposes and oversee the spending. It is beyond the scope of this study to determine empirically the wisdom of this transfer, but one of its purposes is to present the context within which future study is necessary.

This volume thus focuses on revenue sharing as an issue immersed in the policy making process and as a policy that has major consequences for the allocation of public resources. It is not an issue frozen in time. The revenue sharing legislation signed by

President Nixon in October 1972 marked a new chapter in the continuing conflict over the role of the national government in the American federal system.

CHAPTER I

The Making of an Issue

In 1971, $30 billion departed Washington with the high purpose of helping the nation's communities and states solve the many physical, social, and economic problems besetting them. This federal aid was quadruple the amount provided a decade earlier and contributed nearly 20 percent of the revenues of fiscally hard pressed state and local governments. A quarter of all federal domestic spending was going for state and local aid. The money was spent for a multitude of purposes ranging from forest fire protection in Montana to library books for ghetto schools in New York City. It built highways for the motorist and it put money into the pockets of the poor. It did many different things for many different people in many different places. Yet it was difficult to find many people who were happy about this arrangement. Some thought it was not enough money, others thought it too much; some said there was too much federal control of the money, others feared transferring that control to state and local officials; some said too much money was going to the poor who didn't want to work, others said the poor were being shortchanged. Although progress had been made in dealing with many of the nation's problems, there was a general mood that the billions in federal aid had, in fact, achieved little. The highways were as crowded as ever, there were more people on welfare than before, the cost of medical care had skyrocketed, inner city slums continued to spread, and the pollution problem had hardly been scratched. And, despite the increasing aid, many governors and mayors were still in fiscal trouble. They were caught between the squeeze of increasing demands for services and the politically unpopular need to increase taxes whose revenues still fell short of spending. Federal aid was thus a highly charged political issue in Washington, state capitals, and city halls.

The pressure for overhauling federal aid policy was intense, with the advocates of change focusing their attention on revenue sharing, an approach which would provide federal funds to state and local governments without any strings attached to how the money could be used. It was argued that the federal programs had become too bureaucratized, complicated, and wasteful. The only way to reverse this trend was to decentralize some of the decision making by turning some of the federal revenues over to the cities, counties, and states, where officials had first hand knowledge of their problems and needs and could, therefore, make maximum benefit of the federal money. The decentralization argument was buttressed by a fiscal one that pointed to the growing disparity between resources and needs. State and local officials were saying that the federal government could well afford to share some of its lucrative income tax revenues. Federal revenues, tied to the income tax, had expanded right along with the national economic expansion. On the other hand, this economic growth accounted for only about half of the increase in state and local revenues, which were tied primarily to regressive sales and property taxes. It was something of a paradox that between 1964 and 1970, the growth in federal revenues was accompanied by three major tax reductions while, at the state level alone, it had been necessary to levy more than 450 new taxes or tax increases.[1] For these reasons, decentralization and fiscal equity, Washington was under great pressure to return some of its income tax collections to the states, towns, and cities to use as they saw fit.

The argument for decentralization was countered by the view that state and local officials would waste the money or spend it to satisfy the demands of the local groups that could exert the most political pressure. For these reasons, opponents of revenue sharing argued, continued federal policy direction was needed. Further, since it was the federal government that had levied the taxes, it was a companion responsibility to assure that this money was being spent for nationally established priorities. On the fiscal side, if state and local governments were hard pressed, there were alternatives to revenue sharing. A system of tax credits could be instituted that would allow a taxpayer to subtract part of his state income taxes from what he owed the federal government. The states, in turn, could introduce or raise their own income taxes without any net increase in cost to the taxpayer. Another way of easing the financial burden of states and cities would be to have the federal government take over all, or a bigger part of, welfare programs, which were costing state and local governments about $8 billion annually. Federal grants could also be adjusted to require fewer state and local matching dollars, thereby freeing some of the nonfederal matching money for other purposes. In order words, there were several alternatives that might be preferable to "no strings" revenue sharing.

The Environment of Public Policy

These were the basic outlines of the federal aid controversy as the 1970's began, but the issues did not spring suddenly to the attention of those who make and influence the making of policy. Every public policy controversy has an environment in which the dispute is carried on and from which it cannot be detached. It is made up of intangibles such as historical experience and disputed values.

There are also more pragmatic elements such as the next election. The policy environment shapes the views and conditions the conflicts of the institutions and individuals involved. The existence of a policy environment is a given, but the nature of this environment is not necessarily so. Those at the center of the dispute actively seek to manipulate the environment to their advantage. By such manipulation, the contestants hope to influence the larger political world where the average voter is more persuaded by the broad strokes of the argument than by the background detail.

If manipulation seems like an overly harsh word, it is only necessary to understand that issues compete for attention. Policy makers are incapable of dealing with all problems and demands at the same time, even if they were inclined to try. This issue competition is a critical feature of public policy making and is central to the politics of getting problems to government. Several routes have been suggested by which a problem gets on the agenda of policy makers: (1) the result of political campaigns; (2) events pose an immediate threat to a significant number of persons; (3) publicity generates support for action and/or a single individual is instrumental in bringing attention to the problem; (4) problems get to government as a result of policy application.[2]

The political history of revenue sharing showed that it became a major item on the government agenda by a combination of all four and they converged in the late 1960's to make tax sharing one of the most visible policy controversies in Washington. These avenues to government were not systematically coordinated by any person or group, but rather the routes were opened up at different times by separate events and circumstances and by persons acting with different motives. This chapter explores two of the routes by which revenue sharing came before the government. The first was the result of policy application, in this case the evolution of the federal aid system and the problems that arose during the 1960's as a result of the aid programs. Secondly, the threat that the evolving federal assistance posed to different groups by mid-1960 as federal grants started to upset the distribution of political power at the local level through such programs as the Economic Opportunity Act and Model Cities.

FEDERAL AID: EMERGENCE OF PATTERNS

The controversy surrounding tax sharing was shaped by nearly 200 years of history and the intricacies of contemporary American politics. If the national government had never embarked on any aid programs to state and local governments, revenue sharing might never have been heard of. But such was not the case and the emergence of tax sharing as an issue cannot be understood detached from the history of increasing federal involvement in helping states and cities deal with their problems. It is this increasing involvement and the application of federal aid policies that formed the issue environment and generated demands for overhauling the aid structure and replacing it with tax sharing.

Many people object to referring to the federal aid system as a "system," which suggests more forethought and structural coherence than is characteristic of federal aid programs. This objection is close to the mark. The programs of federal aid in this country are the result of recognition of specific problems that arose at different times in our history. The national government responded to these problems with a variety of different combinations of fiscal distributions and policy responsibilities. Some programs brought strict federal controls, others left more discretionary authority to state and local officials. Some programs provided 100 percent federal money, others 50 percent. There was no systematic theorizing about the mix of money or policy responsibility. The absence of a "system" as such is symbolic of much of the criticism of the federal aid programs.

If the evolution of federal aid programs in the United States has not been systematic, it has been importantly marked by a series of precedents that were attached to new programs as they came into existence. These precedents started with the very beginnings of federal aid, which are traced back beyond the Constitution and the federal system itself. In the Ordinance of 1785 the Congress of the Confederation dedicated a section of every township in the public domain to the maintenance of public schools.[3] The first land grant under the Ordinance was made in Ohio, where a fundamental principle of federal aid programs was established. That precedent was the involvement of several levels of government in the selection of the land and the administration of the revenues from the sale of the land. In this particular program the governments involved were national, state, and township. This mix of national, state, and local participation in federal aid policy and administration became the pattern for subsequent land grant programs, which were extended early in the 19th century to help develop internal improvements such as roads. In both the school and the road programs the national policy was to use public land to aid the states, with the states and local governments assuming a role in carrying out national policy.

Along with land grants, the most frequently used method in this early period was the joint stock company, an arrangement particularly adapted for use in the creation of state banks and specific works of internal improvements such as canals. The joint stock company approach created a corporation for a specific purpose with the stock owned jointly by the federal government, one or more states, municipalities, and individuals. Again the cooperative approach was used. About midway through the 19th century the pattern of intergovernmental relations shifted, with the joint stock company falling into disuse and the land grant programs becoming the dominant form of intergovernmental aid. What had been established by the mid-1800's was a system of intergovernmental cooperation, with several levels of government actively participating in carrying out a variety of programs. Consciously or unconsciously, federal aid had begun its evolution of multiple, complex federal-state-local relationships.

As the federal aid programs evolved in the 19th century, several new features were added which became precedents for subsequent programs. First, the federal government began to attach more conditions to the aid and developed the beginnings of methods for federal supervision of the aid. Second, near the end of the 19th century regular cash grants came into existence, bringing with them increased conditions and supervision.

The Morrill Act of 1862 could be considered a benchmark in the history of federal aid. It was the first land grant program to be applied uniformly throughout the nation, providing for grants of federal lands to the states to establish colleges. The Morrill Act could be considered the first categorical grant (a narrowly defined, single purpose grant), because it carried conditions which, by present day standards, seem minimal but which served as a building block for attaching more conditional uses to future programs. The Act prescribed that each state had to maintain a college with a curriculum emphasizing agriculture and mechanical arts. Funds from the sale of the lands had to be invested in safe securities and only the interest could be spent. State matching funds were indirectly required since the federal proceeds could only go for operating costs of the colleges and could not be used for construction. Despite the imposition of these conditions, the hand of federal supervision rested gently on the states. The federal government relied on the states to implement the program and to administer the funds involved, the federal role being confined to assuring that the states met the broad standards set.

It was not long, however, before the federal role began to grow. The opening for new controls came with the passage of the Hatch Act in 1887, providing annual money grants for agricultural experiment stations as adjuncts of the land grant colleges. It was the first time that cash assistance was provided on a regular basis to support a particular program. In 1890, the federal government started to use cash grants as a weapon to force state compliance with its requirements. This came in the Second Morrill Act, providing cash for certain fields of instruction, *with the Secretary of Interior empowered to withhold the money from any school not meeting its obligations.* Before this the federal government had relied on the courts and the states to insure controls and supervision. Now, with the beginning of the cash grants and the rise of federal administrative apparatus, more direct supervision was applied. From these beginnings federal program supervision has grown to be quite extensive. For example, one of the most tightly controlled programs is the federal highway program. From the beginnings of major highway aid in 1916, the federal government has effectively used this program as a lever to force change in state government and policy. When the Act was passed sixteen states had no highway department. Since the law said that each state had to have some central highway organization if it wanted to participate in the program, those without such a department had hurriedly to create one. The highway program also replaced the gentle touch that had prevailed in the federal supervision of assistance. The highway grants were, and are, very carefully supervised and administered. The federal controls were made possible by the system of funding that was established, which provided that the federal grants would be paid as planning and construction proceeded. This meant that highway plans, specifications, and cost estimates developed by state highway agencies had first to be examined by and cleared with federal officials to assure that the states would subsequently be reimbursed. This reimbursement approach has been applied to most federal project grants and has enabled federal officials, to the exasperation of state and local officials, to maintain constant and detailed oversight over many federal aid programs.

NATIONAL POLICY LEVERAGE: MATCHING GRANTS AND INCOME TAX

By the turn of the century, several features had been attached to the aid structure, with primary emphasis on devices to exercise some kinds of broad control over the programs established and funded by national policy. Early in the 20th century major new tools were introduced which held the potential for greatly expanded federal involvement in state and local policy making. One was the matching grant. The requirement of direct matching from state sources began with a forest fire prevention program in 1911 and was attached to new programs as they came along, such as the Smith-Lever vocational education act in 1914 and the highway program in 1916. The matching requirement was linked to the idea that federal aid should be used to stimulate state action in particular policy areas and that this could be best achieved by having the states make a commitment of their own to the program. This commitment was the state matching share of money. If a state was not interested in a particular program it could simply not provide any matching money and would not participate. It was anticipated, however, that the availability of federal money would be a temptation that the states could not resist. The idea of requiring matching funds caused little difficulty at the beginning. A major reason was that it was not much of a burden at first. In 1912, total federal aid was only $12 million and represented less than one percent of state and local revenues. Nearly all of this fell outside of matching requirements, so state and local officials felt no particular distress about the introduction of matching funds. This is no longer the case today.

Federal aid now makes up a much larger part of state and local budgets and officials find they are forced to earmark more and more of their own revenues to put up their share. In 1971 matching funds cost state and local government about $12 billion. This was particularly troublesome to states and communities whose growing budget deficits forced them to cut back their participation in such programs. Such cutbacks were not easy, since they meant that some established programs had to be curtailed, and then the program bureaucracy, special interests, and beneficiaries became restless. Where cutbacks were not possible, governors and mayors claimed they were forced to increase state budgets and to levy new state taxes.[4] A few recent programs have sought to avoid such problems by providing for 100 percent federal payment. One of these is Title I of the Elementary and Secondary Education Act, which provides money to school districts with concentrations of children of poor families. In most aid programs, however, matching funds are required. The matching grant device has not only been used to stimulate particular activities, it is also used to influence state and local policy decisions. For example, the federal government will increase its share of a local water treatment facility if the state will share in the cost, a use of the matching grant to increase the state's role in pollution control. The matching grant, started in 1911, thus came to be a major element in the federal aid and revenue sharing controversy.

The system of controls, supervision, and matching grants would have stirred up few problems if federal aid had remained at the low levels of the early 1900's, but it did not. The Republican decade of the 1920's saw few new grant programs, but it was a period of rapid expansion for activities already being aided, particularly highway construction. In 1920, at the end of the Wilson administration, federal grants to the states totaled just $33 million. The amount of grants continued to grow during the terms of Presidents Harding, Coolidge, and Hoover, and by 1927 grant assistance reached $116 million, doubling to $232 million by 1932. Much of this increase was for major additions to highway aid, a popular program which accounted for most of the assistance funds.

A factor making the increases possible was the ratification of the income tax amendment in 1913. Individual income taxes that year totaled only $28 million, but climbed to over $1 billion in 1918, when rates went up to help pay the cost of World War I. Following the war, collections declined, but in 1925 revenues from individual income taxes still totaled about $735 million. At the same time, revenues from corporate income taxes began to flow into the federal treasury. In 1913 corporate income taxes were $43 million; by 1925 they were more than $1.1 billion.

The coming of the income tax brought a major shift in the sources of federal revenues. In 1913 the largest single source of federal revenues was customs collections, totaling $318 million. This represented about 45 percent of all federal receipts. The next largest item was excise taxes on alcohol, which provided the government with $230 million. The combined customs and alcohol tax collections made up about 75 percent of federal receipts in 1913. These sources of revenue were relatively static. In 1903, customs and alcohol brought in $463 million. Over the next decade they had grown by only $85 million. In contrast, the income taxes proved to be much more lucrative because of national economic expansion. Individual and corporate income tax receipts increased from $71 million in 1913 to $1.6 billion a decade later. Customs and alcohol tax collections became a small part of federal receipts.

The effect of the income tax amendment was to put into the hands of the federal government a sizable amount of revenue which permitted expansion of federal grants during the 1920's and subsequent years. It presented a permanent, vast new pool of resources that enabled the national government to do many things it could not previously do. It also was a source of income that came to be largely preempted by the federal government. By 1970, the federal government was collecting about 90 percent of all income taxes paid by the American people.[5] Meanwhile, the states had come to dominate the sales tax field, while more than 95 percent of all property taxes went to local governments. There thus emerged areas of tax specialization, but the division was not considered equitable. State and local officials began to complain of federal domination of the rich and expanding income tax base, which was linked to a growing national economy, while state and local tax sources grew at a much slower rate. For this reason it was proposed that Washington return some of its income tax collections to the state and local governments to use as the latter saw fit.

THE DEPRESSION: SEEDS OF
NEW CONTROVERSIES

The stock market crash in October 1929 and the depression that followed crippled the American economy. The Gross National Product, which had passed the $100 billion mark in 1929 for the first time in the nation's history, began a sharp descent that did not bottom out until 1933, when it reached $56 billion. The unemployment rate stood at 3.2 percent in 1929; by 1931 it was up to 15.9 percent, and it reached 24.9 percent in 1933 at the depth of the depression.

The unrelieved distress led to an end of Republican control of the national government. GOP control of the Congress, which began in 1919, came to an end in 1931 when the Democratic Party overcame a 100 seat Republican majority and gained a six vote advantage in the House of Representatives. Two years later, in 1933, the Democrats gained thirteen seats in the Senate and also took control of that body. The presidency was added that same year with the inauguration of Franklin D. Roosevelt, ending twelve years of Republican control of the White House. With Roosevelt came the New Deal and a new orientation in American political, economic, and social life. Roosevelt's victory represented not only a new political life for the Democratic Party, it also represented a victory of urban and immigrant America over the rural and nativist sectors. Urban support of the Democratic Party was still in its infancy; it was only in 1928 that the cities had finally passed into the Democratic column. This changing character of the Democratic Party had a great effect upon the agenda of government. The ethnic minorities, labor, and the Blacks outside the south now had some national political leverage; they became an integral part of the new Democratic coalition.

This urban political ascendency coincided with the depression and the New Deal, and so it was no surprise that much of the New Deal program in relief, public works, social security, and labor relations had an urban thrust. This does not mean that rural America was ignored. There were programs to save farm mortgages, rural electrification, and subsidy programs. But the new urban focus contrasted sharply with the rurally oriented programs of earlier years. This new focus was most clearly seen in the area of public welfare. In 1932, while the federal government was providing $191 million for highway aid to the states (mostly rural roads), the federal outlay to the states for public welfare was only $1 million, with Washington spending an additional $1 million directly on welfare activities. But with unemployment climbing and savings disappearing, it was evident that more funds for relief were needed. State and local governments were spending more than $400 million on welfare, nearly triple the predepression level. But this was not equal to the need. As the nation slipped deeper into the depression, the public need for aid grew greater and the states and communities found themselves unable to cope with the problem. Into this growing welfare crisis the federal government stepped in a major way. Federal aid for welfare reached $495 million in 1934. With new programs for relief and public works, federal aid programs reached just over $1 billion in 1934.

A highly significant innovation in the federal aid system during the 1930's was that the federal government began to bypass state governments and make funds available directly to local governments. Traditionally, federal aid was channeled to state agencies, a fitting arrangement for a two-partner federal system—the state and national governments. The new federal funds going to the local governments were funneled chiefly through the relief and public works programs. Washington also became more directly involved in administering some relief and job programs. Both of these arrangements for providing aid had certain advantages of administrative efficiency in that there was a more direct line between the funding source and those in need of help—the unemployed. There was also the salutary political effect that the new Democratic administration was able to cement its new ties with city political leaders by bypassing rural dominated state governments. The direct relief programs also made the presence of the New Deal more immediate to the voter.

The New Deal arrangements of direct Washington-local ties and the direct federal administration of programs were temporary and gradually eliminated. But the seed of a new political arrangement had been planted. It flowered after World War II when dealings

TABLE I

*National Government Financial Assistance
to State and Local Governments for
Selected Years 1902-1974*

Year	Total Aid (MILLIONS OF DOLLARS)	National Aid as Percent of State-Local General Revenues
1902	7	0.7
1912	12	0.6
1922	108	2.4
1927	116	1.7
1932	232	3.2
1934	1,016	13.3
1936	948	11.5
1940	945	10.0
1944	954	8.8
1948	1,861	10.8
1952	2,566	10.4
1957	3,843	10.5
1962	7,893	13.2
1964	10,141	14.6
1966	12,960	15.6
1968	18,599	18.2
1970	23,954	18.3
1972	35,940	21.3
1974 (est.)	44,825	21.3

Sources: U.S. Bureau of the Census, *Historical Statistics of the United States, Colonial Times to 1957*, 1960, p.726; U.S., *Special Analysis, Budget of the United States, Fiscal Year 1974* (Washington, U.S. Government Printing Office, 1973), p.217.

between Washington and the urban areas began to accelerate, much to the dismay of state officials. The new federal-local ties subsequently gave rise to the contention that the American federal system was not composed of two partners, but three—the national and state governments and the cities.

A second significant innovation of the depression era was the introduction of equalization formulas into federal grant programs.[6] The objective of equalization provisions was to achieve a national minimum level of program operations. Since states were unequal in their financial ability to meet the minimum level, some federal grant formulas were varied, giving a greater proportion of federal funds to those states with fewer resources of their own. Before the 1930's, when the federal grant sums were small, 50-50 matching by the states caused no problem. But with the large, new grant offerings in the 1930's and the fiscal plight of state and local governments growing, the traditional $1 for $1 matching was ineffective. The Social Security Act of 1935 contained a variety of programs that for the first time allowed for distribution of aid on the basis of financial need. The equalization approach is an economic redistribution tool to shift resources from the wealthier to the poorer sections of the country. Thus, some federal grant programs became not only a means of stimulating state and local activity, but now also had the secondary function of economic redistribution. The amount of redistribution of wealth achieved through grant equalization is very, very small, but nevertheless the equalization approach became a politically accepted means of assuring that minimal services of targeted national policies were available in even the poorest areas.

Thus, the depression and New Deal period was the watershed in the evolution of the American federal aid system. By the end of the 1930's there had emerged a cumulative pattern of program relations having these major elements. (1) The federal government enacted legislation to stimulate state action in selected policy areas. (2) The programs were cooperative with broad policy established at the national level. Responsibility for implementation rested primarily outside of Washington. (3) Federal supervision and controls were provided. (4) Participation required matching funds.

While these characteristics had evolved over 150 years of federal aid programs before the depression, the 1930's incorporated them firmly into the aid structure and added some new elements that ultimately brought on major conflicts about the grant system. The New Deal programs brought the federal government permanently into policy areas that had traditionally been left to state and local governments; federal officials started to bypass the states and deal directly with local governments; program emphasis shifted from rural to urban problems, opening the way for proliferation of grant programs and increasing costs as the problems of the cities grew to crisis proportions in the 1960's.

THE POSTWAR PERIOD: COMPLAINTS GROW

The twenty-five years following World War II saw the continuing enlargement of Washington's role in social welfare policy making and a great increase in the amount of federal aid going to state and local governments. With this came efforts to reverse the field by seeking ways to reduce federal involvement and to curb Washington's controls over the use of assistance.

The catalyst for the growing national policy role was the same force that had been building up since the turn of the century—increasing urbanization. In 1940 the urban population was 57 percent of the total; by 1950 this had increased to 64 percent and by 1970 it was 70 percent.* This concentration of people put new pressures on state and local finances as more and more funds were needed to provide the necessary services and facilities for the growing number of city and suburban residents. In 1940 the cost of

*These statistics are percentages of persons living in "urban places," a Census Bureau term meaning communities with 2,500 or more persons. Urbanization, as used here, refers to metropolitan areas with a core city of 50,000 or more persons plus the surrounding county and any communities socially and economically related to the central city.

state and local government was a modest $12.9 billion. But the increasing population, the new demands for services, and increasing costs of these services forced the figure up dramatically after World War II. By 1950 state and local spending had increased to $28 billion; by 1970 expenditures were approaching $150 billion. Accompanying this rise in state and local spending was a climb in state and local debt. They were in debt just over $20 billion in 1940; by 1970 their combined debt had risen to more than $140 billion.

The constant pressure on state and local officials to find more money to meet their needs gave rise to more federal aid programs, and this aid became a bigger and bigger part of state and local revenues. In 1950 federal aid provided 10 percent of state and local revenues; in 1971 it was almost 20 percent. The federal proportion would have been greater, but the state and local governments themselves had been forced to increase their own revenue efforts. The consequence of this growing federal-state-local relationship was not increased orchestration, but rather increased harmonic discord. There were three major strands to the discontent, flowing from the fact that certain persons and groups were being hurt from the operations of the grant programs.

First, state and local policy makers and bureaucrats had become unhappy over the proliferation of federal grants and the over-lapping of programs and requirements for aid. The grant structure had become a maze that was increasingly difficult to traverse successfully. Accompanying this was the complaint from governors and local political leaders that the federal programs were forcing them to tie up more and more of their own resources to carry out national policy. This left little flexibility for nonfederal policy initiative.

Second, a new source of friction in the federal system had emerged from the increasing attention given to the cities in aid programs and the renewal and growth of direct federal-city relations. The New Deal and the Democratic coalition had given urban dwellers important representation in national policy councils. This resulted in more bypassing of state government, leaving governors and other state officials disgruntled.

Third, in the 1960's a few federal aid programs took on the additional function of seeking to serve as means for some redistribution of political as well as economic resources. The cities had gained representation in national policy making right after World War II. Now, as a result of the civil rights movement of the 1950's and early 1960's, many citizens were making demands for direct representation in policy making. This was most clearly seen in the antipoverty and Model Cities programs, which provided for giving the urban poor some political clout to counterbalance the political power of the established local government. Alone, any one of these problems would have been a challenge to political wisdom and altruism. But when the three forces converged in the 1960's they brought new conflict into the federal system, giving rise to demands by those who felt the pinch that the entire aid structure be overhauled.

Program proliferation. There were two chief operating forces that accounted for the ever increasing number of aid programs. Part of the explanation was the continuing need and demand for new services, leading to the introduction of policies and programs to meet them. A second aspect was that grant programs rarely die and seldom fade away. The enduring character of federal assistance is illustrated in the Morrill Act of 1862. It was an act conceived at a time when public lands were readily available to support establishment of public colleges. Nearly 100 years later, in 1960, Congress enacted the Hawaii Omnibus Bill subsequent to the statehood legislation and had to provide that the state receive $6 million in lieu of a land grant under the Morrill Act. The sanctity of programs is also shown in the vocational education program established in 1917. It did not undergo a major reexamination until 1963. Then it was expanded. A 1967 study by the Advisory Commission on Intergovernmental Relations (ACIR) of 95 cash grants existing in 1966 showed that 10 were established before 1930, 17 between 1931 and 1945, 29 between 1946 and 1960, and 39 from 1961 to 1966.[7] In dollar terms the hold of past programs was more evident. In 1966, $12.6 billion was spent on aid programs; of this amount $8 billion was for programs enacted during the pre-1930 and the depression eras. The number of individual grant programs steadily accelerated during the 1960's, rising from 161 at the beginning of the decade to over 500 by 1971. What thus emerged in the postwar period, and particularly in the last decade, was a rapid multiplication of aid programs. This in itself was not bad since the need for many services was as urgent, or perhaps more urgent, than when originally established. Proliferation alone perhaps would not have disturbed too many persons, but with the increase came considerable fragmentation and overlapping in the programs themselves. The result was that even the state and local officials eligible for the new funds began to complain about the lack of coordination and the red tape involved in getting the money. The vast array of programs and the complex requirements for applications and project controls were particularly troublesome to officials in the smaller communities, where the bureaucracy was less sophisticated and thus unable to navigate the grant maze successfully. One result was the rise of the "grantsman," an expert in sorting out the federal programs and gaining access to the federal treasury. The more long term result, however, was growing unhappiness with the entire federal aid system. A classic case of overlapping and duplication of grant programs was in the field of water and sewer projects. By the mid-1960's there were four such programs available, each administered by a different agency: the Departments of Housing and Urban Development, Agriculture, Interior, and Commerce. What complicated the problem was that there were no standard matching formulas for the four programs and communities sometimes sought to play one agency off against another. In some cases, the applicant packaged assistance from more than one agency, thereby setting off a coordination problem between the federal bureaucracies involved.

The growth of the federal aid system did not go unchallenged. On two occasions during the 1950's efforts were initiated to develop some kind of coordination of federal and state functions. The Commission on Intergovernmental Relations (known as the Kestnbaum Commission after its chairman, Meyer Kestnbaum) was established in 1953 to find a means of setting out federal and state responsibilities, but when it completed its work in 1955 it made no recommendations in this area. A very specific attempt to divide up governmental functions was launched in 1957 when a Joint Federal-State Action Committee was established to designate functions which the states were ready and willing to assume. The group developed a number of recommendations. One was that the federal government halt its grant programs for vocational education and sewage treatment facilities. At the same time, the federal telephone tax would be returned to the states, thereby giving them the resources to help pay for the new responsibilities they would have. The recommendations were received without enthusiasm. President Eisenhower sent the recommendations to Congress urging prompt legislative action, but no such action was taken then or later. It was evident that reduction of the federal role in assisted policy areas was not something to be easily achieved. Aid programs, once enacted, gain a life of their own and are not easily dislodged. The programs become enmeshed in policy subsystems, each having a cluster of guardians: the Congressional committees that enact and fund them; the federal bureaucracies that administer them; the state and local bureaucracies that receive the funds; and the beneficiaries of the programs themselves. It can be said generally that there is a subsystem for every significant policy area—education, agriculture, aviation, highways, housing, and many others.

The existence and operation of these policy subsystems is of fundamental importance to understanding the politics of the federal aid system. The mutuality of interests between members of a particular policy subsystem and their determination to preserve, protect, and expand their programs and influence not only accounts for much of the incremental budgeting that takes place at the federal level, but also results in tying up significant portions of state and local budgets for matching money. Equally important for understanding the strength and durability of these subsystems is that the line of policy influence frequently is more vertical than horizontal. That is, state highway officials are more influenced by and more disposed to cooperate with their counterparts at the federal level than with their horizontal political superiors, the governor and legislators, from whom over the years the subsystems have gained considerable insulation. The same vertical-horizontal tensions exist at the federal level itself, where the President must compete with Congress for control of the program bureaucracies. These policy subsystems are also important for understanding the legislative process and the fragmented distribution of power in Congress among Congressional committees and subcommittees, as will be discussed in Chapter V.

The existence of these subsystems presents a challenge to those who would alter them. Alteration is made even more politically complex because those who want to liquidate or alter some subsystems would leave other favored subsystems untouched. Thus the state highway engineer may favor elimination of the anti-poverty program to save money, but would leave the federal Highway Trust Fund and its state counterpart intact. At the same time, the local parks and recreation director may wish to divert money from the highway fund to open space and environmental programs. The consequence is that few, if any, proposals to alter aid structures significantly are neutral or successful; there are gainers and losers in all major proposals. Further, it is a political cockpit in which not all combatants are equal. The power of the mass transit lobby is not equal to that of the highway lobby and, consequently, the former has not enjoyed the same continuous successes at any level of government.

Given the nature and operations of these policy subsystems, it is hardly any wonder that there was a proliferation of grant programs in the mid-1960's and that they quickly gained a firm foothold in the political and bureaucratic systems.

City v. State. By legal doctrine, local governments are the creatures of the states and may, theoretically, be abolished by the states. But while this is the fundamental legal relationship between the states and the communities within them, it is not the political doctrine. The Governor of Illinois is not likely to propose the abolition of Chicago government and New York City Mayor John Lindsay could propose secession of his city from the state without fear of any drastic reprisals from his theoretical political superior, Governor Rockefeller. The fact of life is that the nation's larger cities have achieved significant political, if not fiscal and legal, independence from their state governments.

In recent years this political independence of local officials, particularly in the larger cities, has been augmented by the growing connections between Washington and the nation's city halls, a relationship that evolved on a permanent basis in the postwar period. The strength of the federal-city ties is generally attributed to two causes. (1) The reluctance of state governments, long dominated by rural politicians and malapportioned state legislatures, to confront and deal with the problems of the urban areas. The urban orientation of many New Deal programs had been a partial effort to redress this rural bias of state politics. After World War II, national Democratic administrations, with a growing proportion of their political base in the northern cities, strengthened their ties with these city officials and voters by focusing more federal aid on their problems and needs. (2) Federal grant programs shifted from their rural bias toward the urban areas, a shift accelerated in the 1960's with the urban unrest and riots. This urban reorientation was seen in the redirection of federal aid spending. Until the latter part of the 1950's, the thrust of federal assistance was for health, labor, and welfare programs, an orientation coming out of the New Deal era.[8] With the introduction of the multi-billion dollar Interstate Highway Program in 1956, commerce and transportation again dominated federal grant activities, a mix similar to that before the depression. But with the enactment of new educational and social welfare programs during the Democratic administrations of Presidents Kennedy and Johnson, the balance returned in favor of health, labor, education, and social welfare programs. This latter mix of programs clearly had greatest impact in urban areas, particularly in the central cities, where such individual and community problems were most acute.

A result of these new ties between the federal and city governments was a dispute about the role of the states and the cities in the federal system.

The first major outbreak of the controversy came with passage of the Federal Airport Act in 1946. The nation's governors sought to have the program channeled through the states, but Congress wrote the legislation permitting the federal government to deal directly with certain classes of cities. The gate was now open on a permanent basis and the federal-state-local assistance dispute erupted. In 1955, an advisory committee report on local government submitted to the Kestnbaum Commission stated:

> In general the larger metropolitan governments (cities, counties, and special districts) do not like the prospect of being excluded from direct dealing with the National Government. They fear that decentralization from the National Government to the States will be at the expense of the urban areas.[9]

Over the years the direct federal-city programs continued to grow, but the growth rate quickened during the Democratic years of the Kennedy-Johnson administrations. The ACIR reported in 1967 that of 38 programs in which the states had no role, 23 were enacted between 1960 and 1966.[10] The result was a growing belief by some city officials that their salvation rested more with

Washington than with their state governments and that the cities were an equal partner in the federal system.

The new triangular nature of the federal system was argued by Roscoe Martin.[11] Martin contended that while the city is legally the creature of the state, "practice accords the city a considerable measure of independence." Consequently, he felt that any effort to deal with the problems of the cities in the context of the traditional federal system was meaningless. The cities politically had come into their own to challenge any primacy claims of state government. Mayor Lindsay carried the cities' case further in 1971 when he called for the creation of "National Cities" which would make the nation's largest centers legally independent of state governments and establish a special relationship between such cities and the federal government.

The case for the states was set out by former North Carolina Governor Terry Sanford.[12] He feared the alternative to the present national-state arrangement would be a single, centralized government rather than an evolving federalism with the cities joining the partnership. At the same time, Sanford felt that the states must accept much of the responsibility for current problems in the cities and did not feel that the trend toward direct national-city relations had to be reversed.

> It is no longer possible for the states to assert that all federal funds should be channeled through the states. . . . So many local functions are carried on in so many ways with money from the national tax sources that it is difficult, if not impossible, to catalogue everything being done, much less unwind and stop the process.[13]

Despite their differences in focus, Martin and Sanford found common ground in their shared belief that the states had been unable to deal with the growing urban problems because of outdated state constitutions, fragmented state executive powers, weak state legislatures, and inadequate tax systems. But they diverged in their outlooks for effective state action in the future. Martin thought the states had shown little interest in urban problems and would not take the necessary action to cope with them. Sanford, on the other hand, saw the state as the link between broad national policy and narrow local interests.

Whatever the merits of the cases made, the fact was that city and state officials eyed each other warily. City officials were very suspicious of proposals that would alter the aid structure in any way that would affect their direct dealings with Washington. As will be seen in subsequent chapters, this city-state dispute, going back more than a quarter of a century, was a fundamental part of the revenue sharing controversy. City officials particularly feared that such a tax sharing system, as originally proposed, might put them at the mercy of state officials armed with vast new sums of untied federal dollars.

The politically powerless. If state officials felt the emerging federal-city relations were undesirable, local officials were no less perplexed when programs began to go into operation which bypassed them and put federal funds directly into the hands of nonofficial organizations within their communities. Such was the case with the Economic Opportunity Act, under which a variety of neighborhood and other subcity organizations became eligible to receive direct federal grants to operate antipoverty activities.

While there has been disagreement about what was really intended in the antipoverty act, it seems clear that some persons instrumental in formulating the program conceived it in terms of federal government intervention to redress the political balance at the local level.[14] In their view it was a means of giving power to the powerless. Power is a companion of financial resources; therefore, by putting federal funds directly into the hands of the poor, the economically and politically powerless would have the basic ingredient needed to influence policies and actions that directly affected them. This was the intent of some of the designers of the "maximum feasible participation" provision of the 1964 Economic Opportunity Act. Thus, to the earlier functions of stimulating state and local activity, relieving financial hardship, and promoting economic redistribution, there was now implicitly added a new federal policy function—aiding the redistribution of local political power. It could readily be argued that this function has hardly been faithfully served. The limited funding of the program, the internal fighting within many antipoverty organizations, Congressional backtracking on the independence of the organizations and how they spend their money, and the resourcefulness of established local political leaders largely negated some of the intended political change. But there emerged out of the poor neighborhoods a generation of political activists who had come face to face with power and its uses and who continued to press their claims against local government in a multitude of ways ranging from minority demands for community control of local schools in New York City to legal challenges against welfare cutbacks in California.

Participation of citizens living in the affected neighborhoods was also part of the Model Cities program. But after the experiences of the antipoverty program, it was decided that this program would be under the control of an official public agency with the citizen participants having a more advisory than decision-making role.

Regardless, however, of the effectiveness of these vehicles of participation, the critical point was that a judgment had been made at the national level in the mid-1960's that the poor needed to be institutionally structured into local policy and decision-making processes that directly affected them. Given this new function of some assistance programs, an interest developed among the poor to assure the continuation of aid they controlled or in the use of which they had some say. On the other hand, those persons, institutions, and groups feeling the pressure from the political activists had new or aggravated complaints about federal aid policy. To the complaints that had been mounting—too much central control, proliferation, and red tape, rigidifying state and local budgets, state dismay over direct federal-city programs—was now added the charge that the federal government was using its money to upset the established political order. It was into this increasingly tormented environment that revenue sharing entered and became a major issue.

REVENUE SHARING: CENTRALIZATION *v.* DECENTRALIZATION

Perception of revenue sharing underwent an evolution during the period 1964 to 1971, an evolution which is a central theme of this book. Revenue sharing has both economic and political content. As economics, it is basically perceived as a means of redressing some of the fiscal disparities that emerged in our federal system as the national government came to dominate the most lucrative source of revenues, the progressive income tax, and as an equalization tool between better off and poorer states and communities.

At the outset, this seemingly tidy economic logic was immediately confronted with some harsh political realities that were both philosophic and pragmatic. (The tidiness of the economics later disappeared when proponents tried to devise the specific allocation formulas.) The political character of revenue sharing revolves, to a substantial degree, around the complex issue of centralization *v.* decentralization of government. When the prospects of revenue sharing becoming a reality were dim, many of the orientations of Congress and interest groups were shaped by their philosophies on this issue. However, as the possibility of revenue sharing became greater in 1971 (when Chairman Wilbur Mills of the House Ways and Means Committee changed his position and came to support the proposal), the dominant theme became a more pragmatic one of how to divide the money; that is, *some* of the early philosophic and ideological positions were overshadowed as Congressmen turned their attention to the bread and butter political issue of how much money they could get for their constituents. Now, with revenue sharing in operation, some of the earlier political issues and orientations have reemerged and these have become the standards by which revenue sharing is being viewed and evaluated.

In the early period of the issue, about 1965 to 1969, some supporters of revenue sharing saw it as a means of reversing what they perceived as the "growing federal octopus." This view was held by many political conservatives who saw revenue sharing as a means to halt the accretion of federal powers and to return more responsibilities to state and local governments. This political view was closely linked to a fiscal conservatism which saw the growth of federal policy making leading to higher and higher taxes and growing federal budget deficits. Consequently, to this group "no strings" revenue sharing could serve two purposes: returning policy-making powers to state and local officials, and substituting revenue sharing for the growing number of categorical grant programs. The latter would have a fiscal payoff in that the money for revenue sharing would be taken from the other grants.

This view of revenue sharing was not, however, the only one held by political conservatives. There were also those who, while very much opposed to what they saw as a continuing growth of federal power and intervention, held the view that the principles of governmental responsibility mandated that the level of government that raised the money should also be held accountable for how that money was spent. This concept of accountability, shared by some liberals, was counter to the fundamental "no strings" principle of revenue sharing whereby state and local officials would have a free hand in deciding how to spend the federally raised money given them.

There were also those who saw revenue sharing as leading to federal abdication of responsibility for solving national problems. This view of revenue sharing, which tended to be shared by many political liberals, believed that a major function of the national government, but not the only function, was redistribution of wealth, with the progressive income tax providing the largest pool of redistributive funds.

Redistribution policies are those aimed at shifting resources, either in the form of direct transfer payments or services, from higher income groups to lower income groups. Among such policies are income maintenance, low income housing subsidies, antipoverty programs, Model Cities, and manpower training. Nonredistributive policies, on the other hand, are those providing benefits, directly or indirectly, without regard to income levels of the recipients. Examples of such policies are public works, environmental protection, public safety, and defense. Some policies are combinations of both: education, for example, is essentially nonredistributive, but federal programs such as the Elementary and Secondary Education Act and state school aid equalization formulas seek some redistributive effects. The federal government rightly engages in both redistributive and nonredistributive policies, conferring program benefits of varying kinds on all income ranges. State and local governments, while having some income redistribution functions, play a lesser role in this area because of tax resources and the kinds of taxes employed at these levels of government. Thus there is a relationship between the redistribution function and the nature of the tax base. The progressive income tax of the national government and, to a lesser extent, some state governments is more adequate to carrying out redistribution policy than is the more rigid, regressive property tax base of local government. Put another way, the federal government, with its redistribution function, should allocate substantial resources to financing such policies and avoid diversion of such funds to nonredistributive purposes. Revenue sharing must thus be examined in terms of this redistribution function of the federal government. In short, to what extent would revenue sharing, as a system of decentralized decision making, result in redistributive funds being used for nonredistributive purposes? To what extent is such diversion acceptable or desirable public policy?

Underlying this belief in the redistributive function of the federal government was a deep suspicion of the biased and vested interest nature of state and local politics and decision making. That is, many liberals operating at the national political level did not trust state and local officials to take care of the problems of the socially and economically disadvantaged. This distrust of state and local officialdom was not without historical support. In our pluralistic society, organized interests have always been more successful in operating in the political and economic arenas than have the disorganized or unorganized elements, the economic and political have-nots. This is true at all levels of government, but the major advances that have been made by these disadvantaged groups over the past forty years have come about by elevating decision making to the national level. This is evidenced by the social welfare emphasis of the national government since the New Deal. More poignant is the case of civil rights, where remedy could only be found through intervention by national institutions such as the Supreme Court and its decisions on school desegregation and subsequent Congressional-Presidential action on public accommodations, equal employment opportunities, voting rights, and open housing. The history of progress of the economically and politically disadvantaged in the United States since the New Deal has largely been a history of growing federal government intervention and assumption of responsibility.

Revenue sharing was seen by some opponents as a policy that threatened to reverse this progress and recommit these disadvantaged groups to the care of less responsive state and local officials. This long-range perception of the implications of revenue sharing was accompanied by the belief that in the near-term revenue sharing would mean the end of the many categorical grants that had been enacted to deal with some of the specific problems of the disadvantaged, particularly in the cities. This latter concern was intensified as it became clear that the early supporters of revenue sharing were advancing it as a substitute for other grant assistance.

However, just as the conservative view was not monolithic,

neither was the liberal position. Some political liberals, wary of decentralization and approving the redistributive function of the federal government, saw revenue sharing as a means of adding to the total amount of money that was being made available to state and local governments. That is, the categorical grants were needed and should be expanded, but, at the same time, more money should be channeled downward to give state and local governments greater flexibility in establishing policy priorities. To this group, revenue sharing was an expansion, in another form, of federal responsibility for national problem solving. There were poor governments as well as poor people and revenue sharing would help the former as well as the latter.

With the coming of the Nixon administration, the centralization-decentralization conflict was crystallized in the term "New Federalism." The New Federalism proposals contemplated a substantial degree of decentralization of governmental responsibilities, with revenue sharing as the cornerstone. They also included a major, but unsuccessful, proposal to reorganize the national bureaucracy (a threat to many policy subsystems), and partially successful plans to consolidate many categorical aid programs into a small number of broad purpose grants (another subsystem threat). There was no single view on the issue of the locus of policy responsibility since another part of the New Federalism, reform of the welfare system, would have elevated most of the responsibility for income maintenance to the federal level.

In the revenue sharing conflict itself, the initial centralization-decentralization issue, which could not be readily compromised by either side because it was basically anchored in philosophic and ideological considerations, was eventually submerged by more pragmatic disputes that were susceptible to solution within the traditional public policy processes of negotiation, bargaining, and compromise—issues of how much money, how to distribute it, and how it could be spent. It is fundamental to understanding the nature of the American policy-making process and the political scope of revenue sharing to recognize the existence and interplay of the philosophical and pragmatic levels of politics—in this case, centralization *v.* decentralization and bread and butter distribution issues.

CHAPTER II

Politics of Policy
Initiative I

A major characteristic in policy making in the past forty years has been the shift of policy initiatives from the Congress to the bureaucracy and, more recently, from the bureaucracy to the Executive Office of the President. There remain important exceptions to this general proposition, where the Congress has taken policy leadership. For example, during the Eisenhower administration Senator Paul Douglas of Illinois was instrumental in developing programs to help create jobs in economically depressed areas, a program not finally enacted until 1961. In the area of mass transit Congress took the lead, "pushing" the Kennedy administration into support of the first federal urban mass transit program. Congress was also the point of initiation and formulation of policy for the implementation of price controls in 1971. There have also been issues brought to government from outside, such as automobile safety legislation, which gained its impetus from Ralph Nader, and civil rights legislation, much of which was in response to street demonstrations and lunch counter sit-ins in the late 1950's and early 1960's. Policy initiative thus is found in many quarters, both inside and outside of government.

A major point to be noted about the policy process is that the prospects for policy innovation are improved if the idea is embraced by the President and he uses the power of his office to help clear the obstacles. Conversely, where the President is disinterested or opposed, prospects for major policy change are diminished. In any case, the President looms so large in the total process of public policy making that it is essential to any policy study to determine the President's position on the particular issue. The politics of revenue sharing illustrates the critical role of the President in influencing the fate of any major policy proposal.

THE HELLER-PECHMAN PLAN

President Johnson entered 1964 full of confidence and optimism. He had unified the nation behind his leadership following the assassination of John Kennedy and Congress was responding to his persuasion. Legislation that had been stalled in Congress before November 22, 1963, now began to flow out of committees and through Congress. Less than a month after his taking office major programs for higher education and vocational education were before the President for his signature. These were only the advance guard of a greater flow in 1964. A broadened library services program was clearing the final Congressional hurdles and a huge $11.5 billion tax cut bill that had bogged down had gained new life and would be ready for Presidential signature in late February. The celebrated Johnson magic associated with his years of Senate leadership had reemerged in his new job aided by a Congress eager to show its responsiveness to the new President. It was in this atmosphere of public acceptance and legislative success that the President went to Capitol Hill in January 1964 to deliver his first State of the Union Message. The message bore the stamp of the expansive mood of the President, and he gave a preview of his coming budget message, which would not be unveiled in detail for another two weeks.

The President informed Congress that his forthcoming budget would be $500 million below 1964 spending, only the second budget in nine years to call for such reduction.[1] It was a revelation calculated to appeal to the fiscal conservatives, who had been finding little to cheer about in the enactment of new spending legislation. To strengthen the appeal to this group and to display his own brand of fiscal responsibility, he also said he would be cutting the budget deficit in half—from $10 billion in fiscal year 1964 to $4.9 billion in 1965. This budgetary and fiscal optimism of January gave way to a state of semieuphoria the next month with final approval of the tax cut, which the President described as "the single most important step that we have taken to strengthen our economy since World War II."[2]

The tax cut was expected to give a much needed spark to a very sluggish economy. By putting more money into taxpayer pockets, the cut would stimulate a new round of consumer spending and economic expansion. An architect of the "New Economics," Dr. Walter Heller, Chairman of the Council of Economic Advisers, foresaw the further possibility that the new economic expansion would bring more revenues into the federal treasury, in turn bringing on a problem of "fiscal drag." The government's revenues would grow by about $6 billion a year. Unless this cash income was matched by a $6 billion cash outflow, the fiscal brakes would gradually be applied and bring about a new economic slowdown. This was fiscal drag.

While eager to show the American people and the world that his policy was to continue the unfinished work of his predecessor, President Johnson was also anxious to stamp the LBJ brand on his own administration. His receptivity to new programs was demonstrated at the very outset. Within hours of Johnson's taking office, Heller informed the new President of studies under way for an antipoverty program that had received the blessing of Kennedy. Johnson quickly embraced the idea to his own bosom and told Heller to get to work on it. In the process, the program took on Texas proportions. What had started out as a plan to introduce a pilot antipoverty program in a limited number of communities soon became a catchall package of the old and the new that would be spread across the entire national landscape.

There were thus two domestic elements in the air in early 1964. An expected economic boom was in the offing and the White House was occupied by a President seeking to combine programs bearing his own stamp with a policy of continuity. It was clearly a time for the innovative, and it was into this atmosphere that a major new revenue sharing proposal was floated.

It was perhaps natural that Heller would be the source of the new policy initiative. As the early champion of the tax cut and as an advocate of the antipoverty program, he foresaw the possibility that his new idea would make both economic and political sense to a President searching for program identity.

In mid-1964, Heller, who had been interested in the idea of revenue sharing since his graduate study days, floated a trial balloon to see what kind of reception it would get. In a magazine interview Heller presented his views on several alternatives for avoiding fiscal drag, including federal debt repayment, increasing federal expenditures, further tax cuts, or routing more federal money to state and local governments.[3] This latter point was the seed of what came to be called the Heller Plan—a proposal for sharing anticipated growing federal tax revenues with state and local governments to help ease their financial burdens. By attaching the idea of tax sharing to the concept of fiscal drag, Heller's plan became associated at the outset with the idea of distribution of federal surpluses, an interpretation his proposal was never able to entirely shake off despite subsequent fundamental changes in how revenue sharing would work. Seven years later some opponents of tax sharing were still basing their case on the fact that there were no surpluses to share. Heller's initial proposal was very sketchy, calling only for sharing the surpluses with *state* governments with no strings attached to the use of these funds.

Heller's plan caught the interest of Johnson, who appointed a "task force" to make a further study of the idea. The idea of a task force to devise policy proposals for the President was relatively new. The traditional sources of policy proposals were the various departments and agencies which submitted plans to the President through the Budget Bureau. The proposals were then analyzed both by budget officials and White House staff and from this a legislative program emerged. President-elect Kennedy, eager to get started on a legislative program, appointed nongovernment task forces after his election in 1960 to study various foreign and domestic programs.[4] The purpose was to have a legislative program formulated by the time he was inaugurated. Many of the task force members came from the academic community, the aim being to get fresh, new ideas from sources of expertise outside of government. The Kennedy task forces operated in the open and the products of their efforts were made public in the form of task force reports.

Lyndon Johnson adopted the use of task forces in his administration, but there were some differences.[5] Johnson turned less frequently to the academic community in order to avoid charges leveled against the Kennedy groups that they were too intellectually oriented and their recommendations were unrealistic. Johnson also wanted his study groups to work in secrecy. For the most part the identity of members of task forces working for Johnson was not known and their reports were not made public.

The task force appointed to look into Heller's tax sharing plan was headed by Dr. Joseph A. Pechman of the Brookings Institution, whom Johnson appointed at the suggestion of Heller. At the time of his appointment Pechman was opposed to the idea of tax sharing, but Heller wanted him for that reason—it would mean that the idea would get an unbiased examination.[6] Pechman quickly became a steadfast supporter of revenue sharing. The Pechman task force had members from both inside and outside of government. The group finished its study in the early fall of 1964 and sent it to Johnson. The task force members never met with the President personally to discuss the report after it was completed, and its text was not made public. The major content, however, quickly became known. The idea of distribution of surpluses was changed to a plan for setting aside a fixed percentage of the federal income tax base in a trust fund, the money going to the *states* for general aid. The funds would have no strings attached to their use. Heller himself subsequently revised his own proposal, dropping the linkage to surpluses and substituting guaranteed payments,

> even if it means that the federal government has to bear the brunt of periodic deficit financing. . . .The federal commitment to share income tax revenues with the *states* [emphasis added] would be a contractual one, good through thick and thin, through surplus and deficit in the federal budget.[7]

He proposed setting aside one or two percent from each bracket of the tax base for distribution to the states each year on a per capita basis, giving the states broad discretion in the use of the money. He estimated that in 1966 his plan would yield the states about $5.6 billion. He also made it clear that his tax sharing plan was to be *in addition to existing federal grant programs, not a substitute for them.* "To avoid an inefficient allocation of state-local funds, our system of tightly tied aids needs to be flanked by wide-latitude grants like those provided by revenue sharing."[8]

Several features of the combined Heller-Pechman proposals became key points of conflict as the idea of tax sharing moved out of the inner sanctums of the White House into the broader political arena. A major sticking point was that both plans contemplated that the money would go to the states, thus making local officials, particularly city mayors, suspicious of the entire scheme from the outset. In 1965, a spokesman for the National League of Cities, referring to revenue sharing, told Congress, "If we leave it to the States, we are afraid history will repeat itself and the cities will get the short end of the stick."[9]

A second critical point was that the two central features of the plan—sharing of the income tax and unconditional use of the money—were divisible from each other, as became clear over the next three years. By 1967, deficits and tax increases were the major budgetary and fiscal realities, thus temporarily shelving serious consideration of tax sharing. But the second feature, federal aid with no strings attached, came to the fore as pressure was exerted in Congress to give the states more control over federal grant assistance, although the notion was strongly opposed by many Congressional liberals, who felt state and local officials would waste the money if federal controls were eliminated.

Revenue Sharing as Politics

The Heller-Pechman Plan emerged at a time of growing state and local expenditures and mounting debt. It was also put forth at a time of economic and fiscal optimism in Washington. But there was a third element in the environment: the idea was proposed in a presidential election year.

In July, the month following the Heller interview, the GOP held its national convention and nominated Senator Barry Goldwater as the party standard bearer. The Republican platform addressed itself to the issue of the federal grant structure, calling for a "critical re-examination and major overhaul of all federal grant-in-aid programs with a view to channeling such programs through the states, discontinuing those no longer required." The chairman of the Platform Committee was Representative Melvin Laird of Wisconsin, a member of the House Ways and Means Committee, who had introduced his own version of revenue sharing in 1958 and in subsequent Congresses. He was the chief proponent of revenue sharing as a "substitute" for existing grant programs and his views found their way into the party platform.

In August the Democrats met in Atlantic City, New Jersey. They too included a plank, more general, on federal financial assistance, calling for "development of fiscal policies which would provide revenue sources to hard-pressed state and local governments to assist them with their responsibilities." It was a plank that clearly left a lot of room for interpretation.

The candidates themselves, while concentrating on other issues, did state their views on federal aid programs and possible mechanisms for channeling this assistance to state and local governments. Senator Goldwater,in a late October speech in Belleville, Illinois, advocated returning to the states "a share of taxes collected from them. Such grants-without-strings would gradually *replace* [emphasis added] the present system of grants-with-strings, which the Federal Government uses to control more than $10 billion of spending at the local level."[10] Senator Goldwater was thus faithful to the party's position. President Johnson also spoke on the subject, but the sum of his remarks was as ambiguous as the party platform.

On October 27, the President issued a statement on economic issues in which he pointed to the potential danger of fiscal drag on the national economy. He said the remedies included "further tax reductions, increases for top-priority Federal programs, and an increased flow of funds to state and local authorities."[11] While this seemed to leave room for revenue sharing, his next paragraph offered less encouragement.

> The size of these adjustments and the choice among them at any given time must and will depend on the changing needs of our people, state of our economy, and demands of national security—*not on some rigid mechanical formula fixed for years in advance* [emphasis added].

If this left puzzlement in the minds of proponents and opponents of revenue sharing, a second statement issued the following day compounded the confusion because the President endorsed in principle the idea of revenue sharing. A Presidential statement said:

> The national government, as a constructive partner in creative federalism, should help restore fiscal balance and strengthen state and local governments *by making available for their use some part of our great and growing federal tax revenues—over and above existing aids*[12] [emphasis added].

Thus, on October 27 the President said he did not favor any rigid formula for channeling state-local aid, indicating that he was not disposed favorably toward the key portion of the Heller Plan. But on the following day he held out a contrary hope, stating that the matter was under "intensive study."

If the campaign left President Johnson's attitude on revenue sharing in doubt, the questions were dispelled soon after the election. On November 16, Gardner Ackley was sworn in to replace Heller as Chairman of the Council of Economic Advisers. The President said he had tried to persuade Heller to remain; he made no references in the departure statement to the revenue sharing plan. With Heller's departure from the White House, revenue sharing was left without its chief advocate in the inner executive circle. A month later, on December 16, the press reported that President Johnson had decided not to propose revenue sharing to Congress in 1965.[13] Revenue sharing was not viewed with favor within the federal bureaucracy, and labor had made clear its opposition. The issue was up for political adoption.

With Johnson's landslide victory and cool attitude toward revenue sharing, and a new Congress that included many "coattail" lawmakers, revenue sharing was left with very dim political prospects. The issue was not dead, however. During the 89th Congress of 1965-66 the battle lines were drawn and the basic points of the political conflict came into sharper focus.

THE LINES ARE DRAWN

A new policy environment developed during the 89th Congress that intensified the pressure for revenue sharing in subsequent years. Several factors were interwoven in this new setting. (1) The 89th Congress was heavily Democratic, heavily liberal; and during this period, particularly in 1965, there was an outpouring of new federal grant legislation. (2) The first hint of a crack in the earlier budgetary optimism appeared in the spring of 1965 when a supplemental appropriation for the Vietnam conflict was approved by Congress. (3) As the White House chill toward revenue sharing turned colder, the nation's governors became more interested. (4) In Congress, the Republicans became the chief sponsors of revenue sharing legislation, with the conservative members moving to the forefront of the issue.

Stepped up grant assistance. The sweeping election victory of President Johnson in 1964 also brought to Washington a heavily Democratic Congress. The House of Representatives had 295 Democrats and 140 Republicans. In the Senate there were sixty-eight Democrats and thirty-two Republicans. The Congress had a very liberal cast, particularly evident in the House, where the liberals were able to force through a major procedural change to ease the flow of legislation through the Rules Committee, which had been a major obstacle to liberal legislative ambitions in the past.[14] The result was a blossoming of major new grant programs and the expansion of some older ones. When the 89th Congress met on January 4, 1965, there were 135 major federal grant programs. A year later this had increased to 182. The growth was especially felt in the fields of health, labor, welfare, and education.

One of the most notable developments came in education, where, after several years of debate and aborted efforts, proponents of aid to education were able to push through a bill providing for the first time general assistance to elementary and secondary schools, the amounts pegged to the number of children of poor families in the schools. In the first year it authorized more than $1 billion to carry out a variety of education programs. Among other programs enacted were the Appalachian Development Act, the Public Works and Economic Development Act, the Teachers Corps, the Arts and Humanities Foundation, an expanded anti-poverty program, more aid to higher education, highway beautification, rent supplements, and a variety of other new and expanded grant programs. The President's successes spilled over into 1966 with the Model Cities program.

The year 1965 was the high water mark of the Great Society. Less evident was the fact that it was also the seedtime for much of the subsequent discontent over the entire federal aid structure. The great growth of new aid programs led directly to the restiveness over duplication, overlap, and red tape discussed in Chapter I.

The one ray of hope for the frustrated was some evidence that the President was moving toward consolidating some of the narrower categorical grants into a single broad functional category. This occurred in 1966 with the passage of the Comprehensive Health Planning and Public Health Services Amendments, which combined sixteen categories of individual health grants to state health agencies into one flexible program permitting the transfer of funds from one category to another. The White House pointed to this legislation as an "evolutionary approach" to the categorical aid principle. It was, however, a slow evolution: the same idea had been advanced eleven years earlier by the Kestnbaum Commission. The lumping together of these individual health grants was also made easier by the fact that the state was the recipient of the funds in all of the individual aid programs so there was no dispute to settle between state and city officials.

Prospects for more flexible programs were also brightened by passage of the Model Cities program, which borrowed from the concept of the Community Action Program (CAP) of the antipoverty legislation. This provided broad financial grants to revitalize run-down city neighborhoods with local program designers drawing up the specifics of the plan, subject to federal approval.

Despite the CAP, Model Cities, and new health grant approaches, the bulk of the Great Society continued to rely on more narrowly defined programs. By the end of 1966, there were about 375 different grant authorizations. The federal aid system was opening itself for attack.

Mounting budget problems. The budgetary upbeat of 1964 carried over to 1965, when the President sent his new budget request to Congress. "The buildup of our [military] forces which started in 1961 is nearly complete," he said.[15] As a result, the budget called for reduced national defense spending, trimming military outlays to $51.6 billion, $600 million below the previous year. President Johnson also projected a smaller deficit, thus "making continued progress toward a balanced budget." But just a few months later, in May, the first hint of the future appeared when the President requested and received from Congress approval of a $700 million supplemental "emergency fund" to support the growing effort in Vietnam.

With this as the first increment in spending on the Vietnam war, greater needs followed. By the time the President sent his next budget message to Congress in January 1966, the war costs had begun to be set off as a separate item in the budget. The original defense estimate of $51.6 billion increased to $56.6 billion as 1965 dragged on, and his January 1966 request pushed military spending up to more than $60 billion.[16] But even this was only the beginning.

The shift in defense spending began to have its impact on domestic programs and the President and Congress began to engage in the politics of priorities: guns and/or butter. Spending on domestic programs continued to increase in absolute dollar terms, but declined as a percentage of the total budget as defense spending rose faster than the domestic increases. The shifting proportions were shown in the amounts going into the six budget

categories accounting for the major share of domestic aid programs: agriculture; natural resources; commerce and transportation; housing and community development; education; health,
labor, and welfare.

In fiscal year 1966, the total projected budget need was $106.4
billion. Of this amount, $24.4 billion was earmarked for the six
domestic categories, representing 22.9 percent of the budget request. Defense needs were set at $51.1 billion or 48 percent of the
total request. The following year the budget rose to $121.9 billion,
which included $27.5 billion for the domestic functions—22.5
percent, a slight percentage drop from the previous year. At the
same time, defense began to grow with a request of $62.2 billion, or
50.2 percent. The budget sent to Congress in January 1967 showed
the same dollar pattern, but the percentages began to show a
greater break. The total request was $144 billion. The domestic
share reached $30.6 billion, but because of the sharp increase in the
total request this represented only 21.2 percent of the total. The
defense request went up sharply to $77.8 billion, representing 54
percent.

The fiscal environment had changed rapidly between 1964 and
1967. In 1964 an optimistic President had talked about growing
federal revenues and the danger of fiscal drag from unspent
surpluses and about increased assistance to state and local governments. In January 1967, his budget message referred to spending
on domestic programs "at a controlled and reasoned pace."[17] The
1964-65 remarks and actions on tax reductions and balanced budgets were converted in the summer of 1967 to a request for a 10 percent surtax on income and to budget deficits reaching $25 billion.
The budget picture now converted the Presidential chill toward
revenue sharing into a deep freeze.

The President and the governors. If there had been any lingering
hope that President Johnson would come around on revenue
sharing it was dispelled during 1965 and 1966. *The New York
Times* had reported in mid-December 1964 that President Johnson

did not plan to propose any revenue sharing legislation in 1965. This assessment quickly gained credibility in January 1965, when the President sent to Congress his three major messages—State of the Union, Budget Message, and Economic Report. These are the Big Three of Presidential messages and are the major vehicles for a President to outline his major policy plans. None gave any indication that President Johnson was anticipating any proposal along the lines of the Heller-Pechman Plan.

Since one cannot prove a negative, it cannot be definitely stated that the President had absolutely ruled out revenue sharing, but evidence clearly supported the general belief that this was the case. The clearest indication was that throughout 1965 as the Great Society began to take form, the President used the categorical grant-in-aid approach as the major means of channeling increased assistance to state and local governments. A second major indicator was that in May 1965, just ten days after signing the supplemental Vietnam appropriation, the President requested, and shortly received, Congressional approval of a $1.75 billion excise tax reduction. So at the mid-year mark of 1965, the President apparently was not overly concerned about future war costs and major deficits. The major troop buildup in Southeast Asia had not yet started. Any coolness toward revenue sharing, therefore, apparently did not flow from future budget concerns, but rather from his clear preference for the categorical grant approach and the opposition to revenue sharing from important elements of his political support, particularly the AFL-CIO.

But if the nation's chief executive was turning his back on revenue sharing, the chief executives of the states were becoming increasingly charmed by the idea of getting a portion of the national tax collections with no strings attached to their use. In July 1965, at the annual National Governors Conference, the state leaders passed a resolution urging that a study be made of tax sharing. The next year the governors gained direct access to the President and that exchange of views brought further evidence of

President Johnson's attitudes toward tax sharing. On March 21, 1966, President Johnson held a meeting with the Executive Committee of the National Governors Conference and revenue sharing was among the topics discussed. After the meeting the President told newsmen that the governors had raised the issue of "restoring fiscal balance and strengthening State and local governments by making available for their use some part of the great and growing Federal tax revenues over and above existing aids."[18] The President's response to the governors clearly indicated that he did not favor revenue sharing as the means of restoring the balance. "I told the Governors that we were redistributing Federal revenues; we were increasing our distribution to the States." He then recited the record of the growth of the federal grant-in-aid programs during his two years in office and what new programs he had proposed and which had been enacted. It was clear that the President had not moved from his position and did not intend to do so, but the interest of the governors in tax sharing helped keep the issue before the public during the years of the unreceptive Johnson administration. If the White House was turned off about tax sharing, Congress was not, and it was to the legislative branch that the advocates of the idea turned for help.

Congress lines up. Revenue sharing found many supporters in both the House of Representatives and the Senate, but numbers can be misleading in understanding how Congress operates. Congress does its work in committees and subcommittees. The real power of Congress lies in these committees and subcommittees and particularly with their chairmen and senior members. What this means is that no one really speaks for Congress, despite the efforts of the chamber leaders to do so. The real influentials are the committee and subcommittee chairmen, and they speak not for the Congress but for their own particular policy subsystem in which their views are a major influence. This fragmented distribution of power in Congress is the key to understanding the legislative role in the making of public policy. In the initial formulation and legitimation stages of policy making, it is less important how many advocates a policy has in Congress than who they are and who the opponents are. This fact is central to the revenue sharing issue.

The House of Representatives was the focal point of the tax sharing conflict from the beginning because the House must act first on legislation involving federal tax laws. Because of this first claim of the House, it was obvious that those seeking tax sharing legislation would have to make their greatest effort in that chamber. It was clear that the high ground of the battle would be held by the side whose views prevailed in the all-important House Ways and Means Committee, which would have to clear any tax sharing proposals before they went to the floor for action. This meant, in turn, that the views of Chairman Wilbur D. Mills of Arkansas were of the greatest consequence throughout the years of the revenue sharing controversy, and Mills had been a continuous, outspoken foe of revenue sharing. His fundamental position was that the level of government that has the responsibility for levying and collecting taxes should also retain the authority to decide the use of the revenues. The strategic position of Mills and his committee was the single most important fact facing proponents of tax sharing. (Some legislators sought to write their bills in such a way as to bypass Mills by having their bills referred to other committees, a not infrequent legislative tactic. It can be judged that such efforts had at least as much political as legislative purpose.) This was the legislative setting in which revenue sharing was immersed in the mid-1960's.

With the Presidential disinterest in tax sharing came a clear Congressional interest in the issue. A total of fifty revenue sharing bills was introduced in the House during the 89th Congress (1965-66), carrying the names of forty-four House members. In the Senate three bills were introduced bearing the names of nine Senators. There were variations among a number of the bills, but three basic approaches drew the most attention.

(1) *"Substitute" approach.* Representative Laird introduced the first revenue sharing bill in the 89th Congress, providing for a straight five percent return of individual and corporate income taxes collected within the individual states. Laird was not a new entry in the revenue sharing controversy. He had been introducing tax sharing bills into Congress for several years prior to the new interest in the subject in the mid-1960's. Under Laird's approach, what a state received depended upon the collections within the state. The most significant provision of the Laird bill was that the shared revenues would be a substitute for an equal amount of federal grants for health, education, and welfare programs. The consequence of this approach would not be a net increase in funds going to a state, but rather the emphasis was on "no strings" and dismantling some of the categorical grant assistance programs.

(2) *"Add on" approach.* This version, contrasting to that of Laird, was introduced in the House by Representative Ogden Reid of New York and in the Senate by Senators Jacob Javits of New York, Vance Hartke of Indiana, Hugh Scott of Pennsylvania, and Karl Mundt of South Dakota. It did not contemplate that the funds would be a substitute for categorical grant aid, but a supplement. This version also provided an equalization formula to give a larger share of the funds to the poorest states. Another provision required the states to submit a plan for sharing these funds with local government units.

(3) *Education revenue sharing.* A popular version of tax sharing in the 89th Congress was one calling for earmarking the money for educational purposes. Many of these bills were introduced before Congressional enactment in 1965 of the Elementary and Secondary Education Act, which for the first time provided large amounts of federal aid for public education. In all, thirty-two of the fifty bills introduced in the House aimed the assistance at education only. There were two similar bills in the Senate.

From the outset the issue was taking on ideological and partisan characteristics. The new interest in revenue sharing had been sparked by a liberal economist in the inner circles of the Democratic-controlled White House, but the legislative initiative was taken up primarily by Republican lawmakers. Of the fifty bills proposed in the House in 1965-66, a total of thirty-eight carried Republican sponsorship. Twelve measures were introduced by Democrats, and ten of those were versions of education revenue sharing.

More significant than the party labels of the sponsors was their location on the ideological spectrum. A *New York Times* article in December 1964 stated that revenue sharing seemed to have the support of "middle of the road Republicans and Democrats."[19] As the issue developed, however, it became clear that revenue sharing was finding its greatest support from the conservative wing of GOP legislators. This was evidenced by ratings given to the sponsoring lawmakers by the conservative Americans for Constitutional Action and the liberal Americans for Democratic Action. Both groups issue their "report cards" on Congressmen, giving percentage ratings for all members of the House and Senate. The percentage indicates member support for the positions taken by the two groups on particular issues of interest.

The ratings of the ADA and the ACA in 1966 showed a very marked conservative leaning among the sponsors of revenue sharing legislation. Of the 44 separate House members introducing revenue sharing bills during 1965-66, 33 had received high conservative ACA ratings of 60 percent or more. Of those 33, a total of 21 had a ranking of 80 percent or above with five receiving a perfect 100 percent grade. The 33 were also heavily Republican, with 29 GOP lawmakers in this group. The other four were Southern Democrats from Mississippi, South Carolina, and Texas. On the other hand, very few House members receiving high liberal ADA ratings were found among the proponents of revenue sharing. Only 6 of the 44 sponsors had ADA ratings of 60 percent or more.

What was evident, therefore, was that revenue sharing was evolving in the House as an issue that divided along both party and ideological lines, the idea finding its greatest backing among conservative Republicans, with a somewhat more liberal clustering around the Reid bill. The ideological division became more sharply drawn in the 90th Congress of 1967-68 when the issue came into sharper focus as a fundamental controversy between "substitute" and "add on" approaches and members were forced to take a stand on test votes.

The education bill vote. A hint of what was at stake in tax sharing came in the House voting on the Elementary and Secondary Education Act of 1965. The passage of that legislation showed the clear liberal complexion of the Congress and its predisposition to act with dispatch on Presidential legislation. The President sub-

TABLE II

Conservative-Liberal Ratings on
Revenue Sharing Legislation, 89th Congress;
Vote on Elementary and Secondary Education Act

Bill Sponsors	Party	ACA[a] %	ADA[b] %	ESEA[c] Vote
LAIRD APPROACH				
Laird (Wis.)	R	83	0	No
Battin (Mont.)	R	88	0	No
Wyatt (Ore.)	R	68	0	No
Gubser (Calif.)	R	60	6	No
REID APPROACH				
Reid (N.Y.)	R	35	88	Yes
Lindsay (N.Y.)[d]	R	—	—	Yes
Halpern (N.Y.)	R	33	71	Yes
Ellsworth (Kan.)	R	75	12	Yes[e]
Morse (Mass.)	R	48	53	Yes[e]
Todd (Mich.)	D	12	71	Yes
McDade (Pa.)	R	52	35	Yes
Dwyer (N.J.)	R	61	29	Yes
Donohue (Mass.)	D	8	82	Yes
Shriver (Kan.)	R	81	0	Yes[e]

TABLE II CONTINUED

EDUCATION

Matthews (Fla.)	D	50	24	No
Teague (Tex.)	D	80	6	No
Poff (Va.)	R	100	0	No
Bow (Ohio)	R	84	0	No
Berry (S.D.)	R	84	0	No
Derwinski (Ill.)	R	84	0	No
Pirnie (N.Y.)	R	60	6	Yes
Ashbrook (Ohio)	R	96	0	No
Conable (N.Y.)	R	72	6	No
Robison (N.Y.)	R	60	6	No
Bates (Mass.)	R	65	18	No
Skubitz (Kan.)	R	88	0	No
Dorn (S.C.)	D	83	0	No
Whitten (Miss.)	D	89	0	No
Bray (Ind.)	R	100	0	No
Brock (Tenn.)	R	91	0	No
Talcott (Calif.)	R	82	6	No
Wydler (N.Y.)	R	65	24	Yes
Erlenborn (Ill.)	R	67	6	No
Hall (Mo.)	R	100	0	No
Edwards (Ala.)	R	100	0	No
Gurney (Fla.)	R	96	0	No
Pelly (Wash.)	R	75	18	No
Buchanan (Ala.)	R	100	0	No
Cramer (Fla.)	R	93	0	No
Andrews (N.D.)	R	68	0	No
Dowdy (Tex.)	D	94	0	No

OTHER

Culver (Iowa)	D	20	59	Yes
Fraser (Minn.)	D	0	100	Yes
Multer (N.Y.)	D	10	88	Yes
Gurney (Fla.)	R	96	0	No

a. Americans for Constitutional Action. *Congressional Quarterly Weekly Report*, No. 44, Nov. 4, 1966, pp.2764-65.

b. Americans for Democratic Action. Ibid.

c. *Congressional Record*, 89th Cong., 1st Sess., 1965, CXI, Part 5, p.6152.

d. Rep. Lindsay was Mayor of New York City in 1966 and was not rated.

e. Voted for final passage of the Education Act, but on the roll call vote just preceding final passage, voted to send the bill back to committee.

mitted his draft bill on January 12, 1965, giving it high priority. Just two and a half months later, on March 26, it passed the House by a 263-153 vote. In the Senate, backers of the bill maneuvered to gain acceptance of the House version and avoid sending the bill to conference, the graveyard of previous aid to education legislation. On April 11, President Johnson signed the bill into law outside the schoolhouse in Texas where he had first attended classes. The major part of the legislation was contained in Title I, which authorized about $1 billion for 100 percent grants to aid programs in schools with concentrations of educationally disadvantaged children. The program provided for broad flexibility in use of the money.

The vote on the education bill was not linked to the tax sharing issue, but it did provide a clue to the relationship between tax sharing and the federal grant system as seen in the votes of those House members introducing education revenue sharing legislation. There were 32 bills of this kind in the House, introduced by 27 members (some introduced more than one bill); 26 of these members had conservative ratings of 60 percent or more. Significantly, these sponsors of education tax sharing voted overwhelmingly *against* the major piece of education legislation enacted by the 89th Congress. Only two voted in favor of a program that required no dollar matching commitment from the communities and provided wide flexibility in use of the money. In all, 29 of the 44 sponsors of any form of revenue sharing bills voted against the new education program, a two to one ratio. Three additional members voted for final passage but had voted to recommit the bill to committee, and thus kill it, on the vote preceding final passage.

The hint of this relationship between support of tax sharing and opposition to grants-in-aid was substantiated by comparing the overall support of revenue sharing with votes cast on thirty-five grant programs during the years 1965-67. A survey of the House in 1967 by the author showed that 149 members, some of whom had sponsored legislation, favored the principle of revenue sharing.[20] This survey result, combined with 18 additional members who sponsored tax sharing legislation but did not respond to the survey, showed that 167 House members supported the concept. In terms of party affiliation, it broke down to 133 Republicans, 16 Northern Democrats, and 18 Southern Democrats. A total of 54 House members expressed opposition to revenue sharing: three Republicans, 38 Northern Democrats, and 13 Southern Democrats.

The thirty-five grant votes showed a very strong disposition among Republicans favoring revenue sharing to oppose new or expanded grant programs.[21] Three-fourths of these Republicans opposed such grants more than 60 percent of the time during the three year period. Southern Democrats supporting revenue sharing showed an even stronger dislike for the grant programs, with 15 of the 18 in this category opposing the grants on more than 60 percent of the votes cast. There was thus a close identity of views between those Republicans and Southern Democrats favoring tax sharing and those opposing new or expanded grant programs during the years of the Great Society. Conversely, those Northern Democrats opposed to tax sharing in the survey were overwhelmingly in support of the grants, with 34 of the 38 voting for the grants more than 90 percent of the time. Southern Democrats opposed to tax sharing cast mixed votes on the grants, about half of this group of thirteen backing grants about half of the time.

There was considerable overlap, therefore, between friends of tax sharing and foes of federal grants-in-aid. This gave substantive evidence to the fears of opponents of revenue sharing, particularly many Northern Democratic liberals, that tax sharing was being packaged as a device to dismantle the categorical grant programs that liberals had been building up since the New Deal and that were coming out of Congress in great numbers during the 89th Congress. It was not, however, a time of confrontation. Confrontation was not necessary. Congress was in the firm hands of the Democrats, with the liberal wing at peak strength; the President was not interested; labor opposed tax sharing; local officials were wary of it because of its focus on the state. The supporting coalition was composed primarily of GOP lawmakers and state governors. The coalition against tax sharing was in firm control and the 89th Congress ended with revenue sharing safely pigeonholed in the Ways and Means Committee.

CHAPTER III

Politics of Policy
Initiative II

The 1966 off-year elections brought a major transformation in the political composition of the House of Representatives. Democrats lost forty-seven seats in the House, making the party lineup of the 90th Congress 248 Democrats and 187 Republicans. Many of the coattail liberals of 1964 were gone and the House of Representatives became a more conservative body. The change was to be felt in the revenue sharing controversy in 1967 when the issue of federal grants and assistance to state and local governments came to the surface. The positions of President Johnson and his Republican Congressional adversaries came more into the open with both sides moving to address themselves more directly to the problem of how assistance should be provided.

In his January 1967 budget message, President Johnson said the federal government "has a responsibility to examine and improve the grant-in-aid system, making it more flexible and responsive to State and local fiscal realities."[1] Noting the broadened approach of the Model Cities legislation and the 1966 legislation consolidating the health grants, the President said, "In the coming year we will examine other areas of Federal aid to determine whether additional categorical grants can be combined to form a more effective tool for intergovernmental cooperation."[2] The President thereby indicated that he preferred the block grant approach, aid given to finance a broad specified function of government (such as education), to revenue sharing with no strings attached.

Later in the month in his Economic Report the President said he had ordered federal agencies and the Council of Economic Advisers to examine ways of using federal resources in the future when the Vietnam war was concluded. One point specified by the President for examination was "to study and evaluate the future direction of federal financial support to our State and local governments."[3] The President did not elaborate, but the Council, in its accompanying Annual Report, gave an insight into its own thinking on the subject in an analysis of state and local fiscal problems and the growth of the grant-in-aid system. The Council briefly presented the arguments for and against the various approaches to federal assistance. In its presentation, the Council showed a preference for the block grant approach, again citing the health and Model Cities programs as the President had done in his budget message. By the end of January 1967, there was every indication that the President and his advisors considered the block grant approach, rather than fixed sharing, as the preferred alternative to narrow categorical grants.

The Republican Congressional leadership was quick to respond and lay out its own position on the federal grant system. In doing so the GOP leaders moved out on a broader front. The President had indicated that he was staking out block grants as his choice and intended to examine areas where such broadened assistance might be applied. The Republican Congressional leaders went further. They put their stamp of approval on both revenue sharing and block grants as means of eliminating the categorical grant

programs. In mid-January, House Minority Leader Gerald Ford of
Michigan and Senate Minority Leader Everett Dirksen of Illinois
delivered their version of the State of the Union. Senator Dirksen
addressed himself to foreign affairs while Representative Ford
spoke out on domestic matters. In his statement Ford attacked the
grant-in-aid programs

> which keep Washington as the manipulator of all strings. . . .
> Republicans reiterate their support for a system of tax-sharing to
> return to the states and local governments a fixed percentage of
> personal income taxes without Federal control. . . .Tax-sharing
> would restore the needed vitality and diversity to our Federal System.[4]

It was also clear that the GOP did not intend to rely solely on
rhetoric to force the issue. The Republican strategy on the issue of
revenue sharing and the grant system was set out in a House speech
on February 15 by Representative Laird, Chairman of the Republican Conference. Laird said GOP members

> will continue to press vigorously for early enactment of a *general
> revenue-sharing measure to replace the existing grant-in-aid
> programs* [emphasis added]. If the Democratic Members of this body
> fail to see the wisdom of our proposal, however, we will advocate
> block grants in place of specifically tied grant-in-aid funds.[5]

The Republicans thus sharpened the line of conflict in early 1967
by going clearly on record in favor of tax sharing as a "substitute"
for existing grant programs. Recognizing the dim prospects for
getting the issue to a vote, the GOP adopted the supporting
strategy of seeking to convert categorical grant programs into
block grants. It was clear early in the 90th Congress that the
Republican lawmakers intended to seek a limited confrontation by
testing their voting strength on block grants.

If the President intended to preempt the Republican strategy on
block grants, his actions in February and March gave no indication
that this was his purpose. On February 6, tne President sent
Congress a message on "Crime in America," in which he asked for

Congressional enactment of anticrime legislation.[6] The message called for establishing planning and program grants to state and local governments to be under the direction of the Department of Justice. His proposal followed the pattern of the categorical grant-in-aid approach. A month later, on March 14, the President sent Congress another major legislative message on "America's Unfinished Business: Urban and Rural Poverty."[7] The message pointed to a number of areas in which legislation already existed and for which he was requesting expanded assistance. In this second major message calling for Congressional action, the President again chose to ask for expansion of existing grants or new categorical assistance rather than to move toward block grants. Less than a week later the President again addressed himself to the matter of overhauling the categorical grant system in favor of the broad block grants. In his message, "The Quality of American Government," the President noted some of the difficulties in the aid system:

> There are today a very large number of individual grant-in-aid programs, each with its own set of special requirements, separate authorizations and appropriations, cost-sharing ratios, allocation formulas, administrative arrangements, and financial procedures. This proliferation increases red-tape and causes delay. It places extra burdens on the State and local officials. It diffuses the channels through which federal assistance to State and local governments can flow.[8]

He said he had requested the Director of the Bureau of the Budget to make a study to determine areas in which categorical grants could be consolidated along the lines of the health program. "As that review is completed, I will seek the necessary legislation to combine and modernize the grant-in-aid system, area by area." No proposals were made by the President, and while the matter remained under study within the Executive Office, Republican Congressional leaders took the initiative. As a consequence, executive inaction allowed Congressional Republicans to become the partisan champions of both major means—tax sharing and block grants—of revamping the grant structure. From 1967 onward, Congressional Democrats supporting aid based on nationally established priorities and control were increasingly on the legislative defensive.

GOP PROPOSES
"SUBSTITUTE" REVENUE SHARING

Republicans moved out quickly to make tax sharing and the federal grant system a visible issue. Before the end of 1967, 74 tax sharing bills in various forms were introduced in the House. The increasingly partisan nature of the issue was shown by the fact that 67 of the bills carried Republican sponsorship while only 7 were introduced by Democratic members. Equally noteworthy was the fact that the "substitute" approach, which had attracted only a handful of supporters in the previous Congress, now became the major proposal. Two major substitute bills were introduced. One of these was sponsored by Representative Laird. The substitute portion was basically the same as the bill he had proposed earlier—the shared revenues would be in lieu of an equal amount of federal grant money for health, education, and welfare.

The principal substitute bill was introduced by Representative Charles Goodell of New York, a close political ally of House Republican Leader Ford. It called for revenue sharing funds to be derived from a cutback in projected grant-in-aid programs and to be substituted for a portion of existing grant expenditures, although the bill contained no formula or mechanism for making the substitution. The Goodell bill was cosponsored by twenty-five other Republican members, including Ford. The Goodell bill made another departure: it provided that 45 percent of the funds would have to be passed on to local governments. The party leadership had thus decided to widen its base of potential support by building into its proposal a provision to attract support from local government officials. The political aim of the GOP bill was unmistakable. On introducing the bill, Goodell said:

> This proposal seeks to provide for the great public needs of the
> 1960's and 1970's by equipping State and local governments to meet
> these needs. It is an alternative to the philosophy of the Great Society
> which would meet these needs by massive expansion of Federal
> programs and by further proliferation of narrow categorical grant-in-
> aid programs that end up in administrative confusion, waste, and
> centralized control.[9]

If there had been any doubt among Congressional Democrats
about the real intent of the GOP leadership, it was dispelled by
Goodell's statement. It was now clear that the GOP position was
not to use tax sharing primarily to meet state and local fiscal needs,
but rather to use it as a mechanism for abolishing many existing
grant programs and turning many federal policy-making functions over to state and local officials. This policy position spelled
out by GOP Congressmen in 1967 remained at the heart of the revenue sharing controversy in 1974.

Other varieties of revenue sharing legislation were introduced in
1967. A third version was a bill by Representative E. Y. Berry,
Republican of South Dakota. It carried sixteen cosponsors. The
text of the Berry bill was identical to the Goodell bill. The single
difference was that this bill did not specifically state in its purpose
that the funding would be from a cutback in existing grant
programs, which seemed a difference more of form than substance.
In any voting showdown it appeared that the sponsors of the Berry
proposal would vote for a substitute bill. The backers of the Berry
bill had recorded greater opposition to grant legislation during the
1965-67 period than the cosponsors of the Goodell substitute bill.
On the thirty-five grant votes during that period, three-fourths of
the sponsors of the Goodell bill opposed the grant programs more
than 60 percent of the time. The figure for the Berry cosponsors was
95 percent opposition. The Goodell and Berry cosponsors were
also found at the same place on the conservative-liberal scale, both
groups receiving high conservative marks from Americans for
Constitutional Action and low grades from Americans for

Democratic Action. It seemed, therefore, that there was substantial harmony within GOP ranks in 1967 about tax sharing and its purpose. The exception was the Reid bill.

The Reid approach, like the Reid bill introduced in the previous Congress, carried no provision for substitition and was viewed as a supplemental approach like the Heller Plan. Besides Reid, five other House members introduced the same legislation during 1967, two of them Democrats.

In the 90th Congress the GOP thus moved to corner the market on tax sharing. The Republicans had overwhelming superiority in the number of bills sponsored, and they covered the possibilities from "substitute" to "add on," although substitution was clearly the preferred party position. They had also announced their championship of the block grant approach. The ideological pattern that had emerged among tax sharing advocates in the 89th Congress reappeared in its successor. The 74 tax sharing bills introduced in 1967 carried the names of 70 members. Of these 57 had conservative ACA ratings of 60 percent or more while only 10 had ADA liberal ratings above 60 percent.

With the issues now marked out, the GOP leadership moved to test its voting strategy on block grants.

GOP STRATEGY SUCCESSES

In Congressonal politics, there are several opportunities to win (or lose) the legislative struggle on a particular issue. These strategic points of legislative conflict are at the subcommittee level, in the full committee, on the floor, and if necessary, in the conference committee. In the House there is another point of strategic significance, the Rules Committee, which must clear legislation for floor consideration. At each point in the legislative process, at least in the case of major bills, a contest takes place between two coalitions—those favoring a particular bill and those opposing. A fact of critical importance in the Congressional process is that a victory at one of these points does not guarantee a victory at the next, since at each strategic point the participants tend to shift.

At each stage in the process a new coalition must be formed, and this gives the loser an opportunity to recoup his losses. In the House, for example, what you lose in the subcommittee you *may* be able to win in the full committee, in the Rules Committee, or on the floor. It should not be presumed, however, that the opposing groups compete with equal probability of success at each sequential point in the process. Proponents of significant change, independent of conservative or liberal positions, tend to be at a disadvantage at the subcommittee and full committee levels, where they confront the resistance of subsystem politics. When the changes are proposed by the minority party, the disadvantages are even greater. These policy subsystems are likely to be less influential in the Rules Committee or on the House floor, where other forces, such as competing subsystems, ideology, and broader legislative trade-offs may be greater determinants of the outcome.

The first occasion the GOP House leaders had to test their strength and strategy on block grant legislation came in May 1967 when the House took up a bill to extend the Elementary and Secondary Education Act for two years. The original 1965 legislation and the extension bill both carried the categorical approach, although there was more flexibility in how the money could be spent than in most other grant programs. The major section of the bill was Title I, which provided grants for education of the disadvantaged, based on family incomes. The grants were made to low-income school districts with the state acting as the channel for local payments.

When enacted in 1965, the bill stood as a monument to coalition building in the making of public policy.[10] It had gained the support, grudgingly in some cases, of both state and local education officials; it made it possible to channel aid to Catholic schools in ways that were acceptable to both public and parochial school organizations; by being linked to income, the aid had gained general public acceptance as a part of the War on Poverty launched the previous year with the Economic Opportunity Act. Despite the coalition that was pieced together in 1965, the program was a target for change two years later. State educators did not particularly like the way they had been bypassed in the program in favor of local school officials. With traditionally closer links to state capitals than to city halls, it was inevitable that the GOP House leadership would seek some changes to give the state a greater role in the program. Also, by being attached to poverty, the aid tended to favor the constituencies of urban Northern Democrats and rural Southern Democrats. If the state were given more control, it could be expected that the funds might be distributed differently.

During consideration of the extension bill in the House Education and Labor Committee, Republicans sought to replace the Act's programs with an educational block grant to the states, giving the state the authority to decide use of the funds. This move failed in committee, so the issue was carried to the floor, where a block grant amendment was offered by Republican Representative Albert Quie of Minnesota. Republicans contended that state agencies were better able to determine the needs of local children than the U.S. Office of Education, which was dealing directly with the local school districts. The Quie amendment was defeated by a vote of 197 to 168. The vote of individual legislators was not recorded, but the defeat of the Quie amendment was attributed to the fact that the Republicans were unable to split the Democratic vote.

The GOP did win part of its goal, however, when the House voted 230 to 185 to give the state departments of education responsibility for the funds under Title III, the supplementary education program expected to benefit primarily urban school systems. On this vote, a coalition of Republicans and Southern Democrats formed to pass the amendment. Republicans voted six to one for the amendment while Southern Democrats supported it by better than three to one.

The second Republican push for block grants came in August

when the House took up Johnson's anticrime bill, which included grants to support *local* law enforcement planning and innovative law enforcement programs. Republican Representative William Cahill proposed that the state rather than local government receive the funds, the states using a portion of the money at the local level. In short, the Cahill amendment proposed converting grants to local governments into block grants to the states. After some sharp debate the Cahill amendment was overwhelmingly accepted by a vote of 256 to 147. On the vote, Republicans gained Southern Democratic support. The final vote showed almost solid Republican support of the block grant amendment (172 to 4) and the Southern Democrats voting 68 to 14 for it. The final version as passed by the Senate in 1968 provided that all planning grants and 85 percent of the project grants were to go to the states as block grants. This legislation was the first major new bill adopting the state-oriented block grant approach to pass Congress.

The issue of block grants and the states *v.* the cities returned to the House floor in September with consideration of the Juvenile Delinquency Prevention and Control Act proposed by Johnson to overhaul the 1961 program. The proposed changes were community oriented, authorizing grants directly to local agencies. The Act also proposed a form of citizen participation in the program by including the youths themselves in the planning and study of the local program. Once again the local funding provisions of the bill were wiped out on the House floor in what was a repeat of the anticrime vote. An amendment giving the states control over the funds was adopted by a vote of 234 to 139. It was nearly a carbon copy of the anticrime vote with Republicans voting overwhelmingly for the amendment 161 to one. The Southern Democrats voted their support of the block grant 61 to 16.

The first session of the 90th Congress had given House Republicans three opportunities to test the block grant strategy spelled out early in 1967. Republicans were unable to build a majority in the Democratic-controlled committees, but Democratic control did not prevail on the floor, where new influences were brought to bear and new coalitions were built to override committee action.

The GOP strategy did not wholly succeed on the education bill, when the Southern Democrats stayed with their fellow party members from the north and the Johnson administration to defeat the major block grant amendments. The nature of the program made it in the self-interest of the Southern Democrats, who frequently represented poor rural districts, to retain the existing formula. Any change in the formula for distribution also threatened to reopen the religious issue and perhaps kill the program. Their self-interest was not a factor in the anticrime and juvenile delinquency programs or in the block grant amendment on supplemental education centers. On these the Southern Democrats broke ranks and voted with the Republicans against the position of the House Democratic leadership and the Johnson administration. In the case of the anticrime and juvenile delinquency grants, both of these programs seemed to Southern Democrats to benefit primarily urban areas where both crime and juvenile delinquency had their greatest concentrations. These programs also seemed to aim at problems associated with urban blacks. Given this focus, it was clearly in the interest of most Southern Democrats to support the GOP amendments, which gave more discretionary authority to state officials to distribute the money. The expectation was that nonurban districts would thereby be able to receive a portion of the money. This expectation paid off, and it subsequently became one of the major complaints of city officials that the anticrime funds were being allocated by the states without regard to the special needs of the cities, where the incidence of crime was the greatest.

During the 90th Congress the Johnson administration and its Congressional supporters, in continuing to rely on the categorical grant approach, were forced on the legislative defensive on the general issue of changing the aid system and on the particular issue of block grants to the states. In the process the conservative coalition of Republicans and Southern Democrats reformed, and the issue of federal aid became entangled with the city *v.* state controversy. It was now clear to legislators from urban centers that their best strategy would be to keep the issue of block grants and revenue sharing locked up in Congressional committees. However, in some cases this might not be possible, since not all House committees were as liberal or urban oriented in their membership as the Education or Labor and Judiciary Committees. In more conservative committees, this strategy had less chance of success. In these committees, opponents of block grants would have to rely on subsystem resistance to any proposals that radically altered the operations of the subsystem. In either case, a floor fight put opponents of block grant aid on perilous ground. The Southern Democratic group held the swing vote, and it was clear that a heavy majority was disposed toward the GOP position. Since there was a link between the block grant and revenue sharing issues, it looked like the foes of revenue sharing would face the same peril on the floor.

Pressures Outside of Congress

While the revenue sharing and block grant controversy was taking form in Congress, interest in revenue sharing was growing off Capitol Hill. If the sharing legislation itself was safely entombed in the House Ways and Means Committee, it was not so dead in the outer world.

The governors continued their pressures for revenue sharing, while the mayors remained interested in the money but suspicious of the approach because of the states' identification with sharing. Then a major convert to the cities' position came forth in the person of Governor Nelson Rockefeller of New York. In early 1967 Rockefeller asserted the clear view that the state would be the proper recipient of the shared revenues. His stand put him in direct opposition to New York City Mayor John Lindsay, who made it equally clear that he favored direct payments to the cities. Later that year, in an effort to achieve a city-state political alliance behind revenue sharing, the Governor modified his stand to include the cities as direct recipients. He said a joint state-local effort was the only hope for approval of tax sharing. Mayors, meanwhile, remained wary. On February 6, a spokesman for the National League of Cities told a Senate subcommittee that the states could not be trusted to meet urban needs and therefore cities were very leery about revenue sharing.[11] Mayor John Collins of Boston called it the "most dangerous idea in America today."

While the governors and mayors were eying each other cautiously, efforts were being made by others to write a state-local settlement into a formal revenue sharing plan. This came during mid-summer hearings by the Subcommittee on Fiscal Policy of the Joint Economic Committee, which held hearings on the issue of tax sharing.[12] This committee is not a legislative committee and had no jurisdiction over revenue sharing legislation, but it does carry considerable prestige as an expert committee on economic and fiscal matters, and its hearings can, therefore, give useful exposure to an issue. Among the witnesses were Heller and Pechman. By this time the issue of whether the state and/or local governments should receive funds directly had become heated. In recognition of the state-local split, Heller presented several possible ways of assuring that a portion of any shared revenues would go to local governments. One of his suggestions was along the lines of the Javits-Reid approach whereby the states would develop plans for passing on a part of the revenues to local governments. He also said that a minimum guarantee for local units—for example, 40 percent—could be written into any legislation to prevent the states from stopping the flow of funds. He added, however, that a fixed percentage had a disadvantage in that the degree to which states delegate responsibilities to local units varied greatly. The issue was not resolved for two years.

Another major forum for revenue sharing was the Advisory

Commission on Intergovernmental Relations. The Commission was established by Congress in 1959 to study the problems of relations between federal, state, and local levels of government and to make recommendations on solutions to the problems. The Commission has twenty-six members. Three are appointed by the Vice President, 3 by the Speaker of the House, and 20 are chosen by the President from several categories including the general public, the federal executive branch, and various classes of state and local officials. Of the 26, a majority of 14 is made up of governors, mayors, members of state legislative bodies, and elected county officials. The Commission is, therefore, weighted in numbers toward nonfederal officials.

In early 1967 the Commission said a major study was under way focusing upon the possibilities for strengthening the financial resources of state and local governments. One of the possibilities to be studied was tax sharing. In October the Commission met to approve the proposals generated by the study. Among the recommendations adopted by the Commission was support for both revenue sharing and block grants. Newspaper accounts of the meeting pointed out that Commission Chairman Farris Bryant, director of the Office of Emergency Planning for President Johnson, dissented from the Commission action.[13] It was also noted that two cabinet officer members did not attend the meeting—Treasury Secretary Henry H. Fowler and Attorney General Ramsey Clark. It was evident that the official White House position remained opposed to revenue sharing and the President was not going to be pressured into any change of position. In its annual report for 1967 the Commission described its recommendations as "middle of the road." This seemed an accurate appraisal of its policy recommendations—the report urged broadened categorical grants, functional block grants, and general support of revenue sharing. In an effort to bridge the gaps between the diverse positions, the Commission supported all three possibilities in what it called a "fiscal mix."

The year 1967 also brought stirrings from the grass roots. State legislatures were passing resolutions calling for action on tax sharing. Such resolutions came from North Dakota, Iowa, Illinois, South Dakota, Missouri, Colorado, Florida, and Texas. These state legislative resolutions showed the same divided opinion found in Congress between revenue sharing as a substitute for grants-in-aid and as a supplemental means of channeling financial assistance to state and local governments. The Iowa resolution endorsed the principle of revenue sharing "to partially or wholly offset federal categorical grant-in-aid programs which now exist or may be developed in the future." The Texas legislature, on the other hand, made it clear that it contemplated that revenue sharing funds "shall be in addition to any other federal grant programs which may be enacted by the Congress." At the man-on-the-street level, a January 1967 Gallup Poll showed that 70 percent of the American public favored tax sharing while only 18 percent opposed it.

1968 ELECTION: REVENUE SHARING WINS

Pressures were surfacing in many places in 1967 for some kind of action on tax sharing. But the rumblings of that year were calmed in election year 1968. In the "time of troubles" of 1968, less emotionally charged issues like tax sharing were eclipsed. Two assassinations, riots in over a hundred cities after Martin Luther King's shooting, and the Chicago convention riot had created a new kind of issue environment in which revenue sharing could not compete. It was clear, nevertheless, from the Presidential campaign of 1968 that tax sharing, while not a major issue, had arrived at a major new junction in its political history.

No matter who won the election the White House would be occupied by a President openly in support of revenue sharing. For the Democratic candidate, Vice President Hubert Humphrey, this represented a major modification of an earlier stand he had taken as the number two man to President Johnson. In 1966, Humphrey

had accused proponents of tax sharing of "oversimplifying" the issue of aid to states, saying the federal government could not just
ladle out money to prop up weak, obsolete, and ineffective state
and local governments. "Federal aid to be effective must be
managed and used in a political and social environment that is
conducive to action."[14] He emphasized the states' lack of organization and their consequent lack of ability to act effectively. But in
the summer of 1968, Humphrey was on his own and free to modify
earlier stands on tax sharing. Among Humphrey's close advisors
during the campaign was Walter Heller.

By mid-August Humphrey was showing a favorable disposition
toward revenue sharing. He was calling for looser controls between
Washington and state and local government, suggesting that one
way of achieving this might be some form of revenue sharing. As
the campaign continued his views became more clear, and by the
end of October he was on record for a revenue sharing program of
$5 to $10 billion a year.

Republican candidate Richard Nixon was also in favor of tax
sharing. Nixon said:

> Generally, I favor a no-strings approach to the sharing of Federal
> tax revenues with local and state governments. . . .
> The whole point of a tax sharing program is to take advantage of
> both the Federal Government's power and efficiency as a tax collector
> and the state and local governments' efficiency and effectiveness as
> problem solvers. But if we are to truly gain the latter advantage, then
> we cannot make the Federal directives too specific lest we tie the hands
> of administrators at the local level. We can stipulate the general
> purposes of any so-called block grants, but we should attach very few
> specific strings.[15]

It was evident from the 1968 campaign that revenue sharing,
which had been lying moribund in the House Ways and Means
Committee, was to gain a new lease on life. This in no way reduced
the strategic significance of the Ways and Means Committee, but it
did mean that a radical change in the coalition supporting tax
sharing had occurred. State and local officials seeking a revenue

sharing program could now look to the White House to act as the political broker between the various factions favoring such sharing. Before 1969 there was no single person with sufficient influence to settle the differences between members and potential members of the coalition, particularly the antagonisms between the governors and the mayors and the issue of "substitute" *v.* "add on." This situation was now fundamentally changed. The political elevation of revenue sharing helped its advocates, because the issue now could be boosted by the prestige and influence of the Presidential office. At the same time, the GOP legislative strategists in Congress could no longer determine alone how the issue and policy would be formulated and what legislative strategies would be employed. Their role was now secondary to that of the President, and they would have to seek their objectives through a coalition controlled by the White House. The policy initiative shifted to the President.

CHAPTER IV

Building a Coalition

The formulation of a revenue sharing program had been going on for five years, but since there was no single source of policy leadership on the issue, there were a number of alternatives and combinations. There were "substitute" bills, "add on" versions, and bills that earmarked funds for special purposes. Some would give money only to the states, others would include both state and local governments. Each version had its band of supporters, but there was no proposal commanding majority support. Now, however, for the first time, the President was to take over the policy leadership and the winnowing process was to begin. Those in charge of formulating the Presidential version had to look ahead to the crucial process of getting the bill through Congress. To have any chance the formulators needed the broadest possible coalition of supporters. This was the situation that faced the new administration even before it took office in January 1969.

President-elect Nixon was quick to take the GOP policy leadership. A task force to examine problems and propose policies, a mechanism adopted by President Kennedy which flowered under

President Johnson, was now the accepted way for a chief executive to go outside the bureaucracy for policy innovation or to give the appearance of innovation. Richard D. Nathan was named to lead an Intergovernmental Fiscal Relations Force to look into revenue sharing. Nathan had been involved in revenue sharing studies for several years. He had written his doctoral dissertation at Harvard on the subject, had drawn up legislation for Representatives Laird and Goodell a few years earlier, and had worked at Brookings Institution with Pechman. A few weeks after the election Nathan submitted a thirty-three-page report to the President-elect in which he cited the need for revenue sharing both as a *fiscal* tool to help state and local governments and as a *political* tool to decentralize public policy decision making.[1]

Meanwhile, a second task force was arriving at a similar conclusion. This was the Task Force on Urban Affairs, headed by Edward G. Banfield, professor of government at Harvard.[2] Banfield was identified with more conservative, *laissez-faire* notions about the useful extent of the federal government's role in dealing with social problems. It could hardly have been a surprise then that a major finding of this Task Force also was a recommendation, similar to previous proposals, that a system of federal revenue sharing be established which de-emphasized the role of the federal government in intergovernmental policy making. Both the Nathan and Banfield approaches to revenue sharing were similar to the Pechman report of 1964. The big difference was that while President Johnson never endorsed the findings of his group, President Nixon was clearly on record favoring a revenue sharing scheme.

The President-elect also fell heir to a third report advocating revenue sharing. In January 1967, acting on a Congressional authorization, President Johnson had appointed a National Commission on Urban Problems, headed by former Senator Paul Douglas of Illinois.[3] The Commission's recommendations were sent to President Johnson just a month before he left office. Among the proposals was one to establish a system of revenue sharing with state and local governments. But the Douglas report had some new twists. A major point was that none of the shared revenues would go to communities with fewer than 50,000 persons. One aim of this was to encourage small communities in a metropolitan area to consolidate their governments into larger units and thereby qualify for the new federal money. The report also pointed out the necessity of strengthening state governments so they could play a more effective role in solving urban problems.

Politically, the reports had a balance. Two came from Nixon's own task forces, advocating a reduced federal policy role, while the Douglas report was the product of a commission headed by a Democrat long identified with economic liberalism and strong central government. In sum, as the new President took office, he had a campaign commitment to revenue sharing buttressed by a personal and party philosophy favoring a diminished national policy role. In addition, he had three fresh reports advocating tax sharing. If this was not enough, he now had among his top advisors Representative Laird (as Secretary of Defense), who had been among the earliest Congressional proponents of revenue sharing and who was now supporting the plan at Cabinet meetings.

Nixon's case for tax sharing was strengthened externally by the growing financial crisis at the state and local levels. From the end of World War II into the early 1950's state and local debt had increased at the rate of about $3 billion a year; from about 1953 to 1958, debt began to climb roughly $5 billion annually. The rate of acceleration continued to increase, and by the mid-1960's, state and local debt was rising at the rate of $7 billion a year. But this was not the end. Beginning in 1966, the increase in debt had soared to an annual rate of more than $10 billion, as state and local governments were caught between the dual pressures of inflation and inadequate tax resources. The pressure was especially intense in the major cities, where the costs were going up and income from the tax base, chiefly revenues from property tax, was lagging behind. More and more middle class residents were making their exodus to the suburbs, leaving the cities with increasing numbers of low-income citizens who required more services but paid fewer taxes. State and local revenues were further eroded when the 1969-71 recession reduced tax receipts. The result was that local officials found it necessary to raise taxes or cut services, and in many cases, to do both. The adjustments came in such varied forms as fewer public building projects, cuts in rubbish collections, and the layoff of public workers.

The resulting political scenario was vividly portrayed in New York. Mayor John Lindsay sent a message to Governor Rockefeller in late 1968, requesting an extra half billion dollars in state aid for New York City. The Governor's response to Lindsay and other local officials in the state was a call for a 5 percent cut in projected state aid for schools, welfare, pay raises, and other programs. But the Governor's response, in the form of his annual message to the state legislature, was addressed not only to legislators and local officials in the state, but also to the man who was about to take over the White House. If Rockefeller was telling his local leaders that the state was in fiscal trouble, he was also telling the President-elect that he was not going to allow the buck-passing to stop in Albany; he intended to carry his problem right to the door of the White House. And so he did. From mid-January to mid-February, Rockefeller was busily conferring with the new President, White House officials, and the state's Congressional delegation about the need for more federal money. The biggest item the Governor pushed was indefinite continuation of the 10 percent federal income tax surcharge and return of some of the proceeds to the state and local governments for education. The White House showed little enthusiasm. The upshot of the situation was that President Nixon entered office as state and local officials were starting to bend under the fiscal crunch and were urgently sending out signals that they did not intend to bear the total political brunt of the problem; they intended to share their political troubles with Washington.

But if the messages going up had a crisis tone, the messages coming back from the White House were more cautious. The President was not going to be pushed hastily into a firm policy decision on tax sharing. The reasons for Presidential reticence were twofold. First, the new administration had not yet formulated a revenue sharing plan that was ready for Congress. To get his program together, Nixon established an interagency committee which included Arthur F. Burns, Counsellor and chief economic advisor to the President; Murray L. Weidenbaum, newly appointed Assistant Secretary of the Treasury for Economic Policy; and Nathan, now serving as an Assistant Director of the Bureau of the Budget. Other members of the committee came from the White House staff and the Council of Economic Advisers. The committee brought in a number of other representatives as the bill was being put together, but the prime responsibility fell to Weidenbaum in the Treasury Department, who served as chairman of the administration's new Task Force on Revenue Sharing, and Nathan, with Burns providing the link between the committee and the President.

The second reason for moving cautiously was linked to the first. That is, if the governors and mayors were inclined to pass the buck upward, they had better resolve the differences between themselves about how any shared revenues would be divided, so that the final bill would be a consensus package that all could get behind when it was sent to Congress. It became the task of the committee formulating the bill to play the broker role between state and local executives.

Playing peacemaker between the governors and local officials was a sensitive matter, since the Nixon administration was already off to a shaky start as a mediator of state-local disputes. In February it was announced that Nixon was establishing a new Office of Intergovernmental Relations to serve as the liaison between

Washington and state and local governments. If the idea of such an office generally appealed to governors and mayors, many local officials were skeptical of the fact that the office would be headed by Vice President Spiro Agnew, a former governor and a person who had not especially endeared himself to big city mayors, many of them Democrats, during the recent Presidential campaign. The mayors became even more suspect of the new arrangement when Agnew appointed another former governor, Nils Boe of South Dakota, as director of the new office. It appeared to the mayors from the outset that the Nixon administration was more attuned to state governors than to city mayors and that the attention enjoyed during the Kennedy-Johnson years was now at an end. The potential for the new alignment was heightened by the fact that two-thirds of the nation's governors were Republican. Despite this skepticism, the governors and the mayors wanted money and the President was committed to revenue sharing. One of the first needs, therefore, was to get a political settlement between the governors and the local officials that would boost the possibilities for Congressional acceptance of tax sharing. It was clear that only Presidential leadership would finalize such a settlement. Meanwhile, the imprint of Presidential policy leadership on revenue sharing was already evident in the new Congress.

CONGRESS HOLDS BACK

At the beginning of each new Congress, most Congressmen automatically reintroduce bills that did not get enacted into law during the previous Congress. Consequently, there is a torrent of bills flowing into the legislative hopper in the beginning days. In some cases, prospects are no brighter than before, but bills are resubmitted for their publicity value back home or to satisfy a particular group seeking the legislation. In other cases, such as revenue sharing, they are reintroduced in hopes that support has grown sufficiently to get the bill enacted into law.

This was the case in the opening days of the 91st Congress, January 1969. Revenue sharing legislation was included among the thousands of bills proposed in the House during the opening weeks. But there was a noticeable difference this time. There were not quite as many tax sharing bills going into the hopper and, more importantly, the House GOP leaders were not among the sponsors. GOP policy leadership had shifted from the Congress to the White House, and the Republican leadership was waiting for their new President to lead the way on the issue. The Congressional leadership bill of the previous Congress, the Goodell "substitute" proposal, was virtually forgotten, as it had become evident that the President would propose revenue sharing as an "add on" and not a substitute for existing grant-in-aids. There was, in fact, no bill from the GOP leadership in the House prior to the President's own plan, which was not to be made public until midsummer. Before the President's proposal, just over 40 revenue sharing bills were introduced into the House, carrying 55 names, 38 of them Republican. Only five Republican Congressmen introduced substitute legislation in the opening of the new Congress. An interesting feature of the bills that were introduced was that a handful of them had adopted the approach of the Douglas Commission, limiting shared revenues to communities with populations over 50,000. As had become the practice, nearly all the House bills went to the Ways and Means Committee, the graveyard of previous revenue sharing bills. The only exceptions were three bills which went to the Government Operations Committee because their funding feature was tied in with improving intergovernmental relations, a responsibility of that committee.

In the Senate, GOP members did not wait for the President, but moved to introduce their own legislation. The need for restraint was less important in the Senate. It was the House that would have to take the first step on the tax sharing plan, and it was in the House that revenue sharing faced its greatest obstacles. The GOP members of the lower chamber wanted to settle on a unified position before making their move, and that position would await a Presidential decision. Also, the Senate had not followed the earlier House GOP lead on "substitute" revenue sharing. One of the illuminating aspects of the activity in the Senate was the position of now-Senator Charles Goodell, whom Governor Rockefeller had appointed to replace assassinated Senator Robert Kennedy. Goodell, while in the House, had been at the forefront of the "substitute" approach to revenue sharing. He now underwent a transformation. He took over the representation of a much broader constituency and owed his position to one of the major proponents of revenue sharing. Soon after the session began Goodell introduced a new revenue sharing plan. In introducing his bill on January 15, Goodell said his proposal was based on the revenue sharing plan he had sponsored in the House two years earlier.[4] What he did not say, however, was that he had made a significant change. Instead of proposing tax sharing as a substitute for existing grants, Goodell now was specifically offering his plan as a supplement to the existing federal grants, a position compatible with what was evolving in the White House and with the approach of Rockefeller. A change he did acknowledge was adoption of the Douglas formula on population.

In the Douglas formula, the larger urban areas were given greater consideration in the distribution of any shared revenues. But, it should be noted, this "victory" of the larger urban areas was not a triumph over the state, but over communities with less than 50,000 population. In only two states, New York and Maryland, would the cities come out on top of the states in the amount they would receive.[5] The New York Senator's formula was fine for the cities of New York, but was not as beneficial for cities in neighboring Connecticut, for example. In New York, urban areas would receive 73 percent of the state's share, with only 27 percent going to the state government. In Connecticut, on the other hand, the state was to receive nearly 71 percent of the money with only 29 percent going to the cities. In some states where there were only one or two eligible urban areas, the bulk of the money would go to the state. In Arkansas, the state government would receive nearly 96 percent of the money; in Idaho, 97 percent; Maine 94. In all, there were twelve states in which more than 90 percent of the state's share would stay with the state rather rather than with local government. Nationwide, the state governments would receive 66 percent of the money, the urban areas 34 percent. The upshot of this urban approach was that the small local governments were effectively eliminated from participation. If the small communities were to be dealt back into the game, either the states would have to give up some of their money or the larger urban areas would lose their favored position and see some of their share go to the small towns and villages. As an approach to urban fiscal needs, the Goodell proposal had merit, but politically it excluded too many persons needed to build support for the program.

Goodell was not the only Senator taking a new look at revenue sharing. Another was Senator Edmund Muskie of Maine. Two years earlier, in 1967, Muskie had shown a clear chill toward revenue sharing during hearings by his Subcommittee on Intergovernmental Relations. During the hearings, Muskie pointed out to witnesses that Senate backing for revenue sharing was coming from persons from whom he was unable to get support for federal aid bills. "When I find that tax sharing has that kind of support, I've got to be suspicious of it."[6] Muskie's suspicions apparently were allayed by 1969, as revenue sharing gained more and more political steam. In June Muskie introduced a bill, the "Intergovernmental Revenue Act," that would combine revenue sharing and tax credits as twin devices for aiding local governments.[7] The revenue sharing portion was very close to the provisions of the Goodell bill (Goodell also cosponsored the Muskie plan), channeling a greater share of the funds to the larger municipalities. Muskie, chairman of the Intergovernmental Relations Subcommittee, had his bill referred to the parent Government Operations Committee rather than to the Senate

Finance Committee. The Government Operations Committee, in turn, referred it to his subcommittee. In this way he was in a position to hold hearings on tax sharing without waiting for action in the House of Representatives, thus giving revenue sharing the forum it had been unable to get in the House Ways and Means Committee. Prior to Senate floor action, however, the Senate Finance Committee would have to consider any bill, and it was clear that the Finance Committee would wait for action by the House. It was evident that, regardless of any maneuvering on committee referral and friendly hearings, revenue sharing proposals were under the initial jurisdiction of the House Ways and Means Committee, and unless that committee acted, tax sharing was dead.

The Goodell and Muskie bills were indicative of the political evolution of the issue, but the major Senate tax sharing bill was one introduced by Republican Senator Howard Baker of Tennessee. The Baker bill was cosponsored by twenty fellow Republicans, including Senator Goodell.[8] It was referred to the Finance Committee, which normally handles tax legislation. The Baker bill was also an add-on version, but it did not limit the sharing by population. Funds would be shared with all states, counties, municipalities, towns, and villages. The bill treated the large urban areas less favorably than the Goodell bill. It was designed to have the widest possible political appeal.

Regardless of the differences in approach, two things were clear. First, substitute proposals no longer had significant open political support, either in the Congress or in the White House. Despite this apparent shift from the substitute to the supplementary approach, however, revenue sharing opponents were still unpersuaded—the clear possibility remained that revenue sharing, if established, could siphon funds away from other grant programs if pressures developed for more and more "no strings" money or if major federal budgetary imbalances continued. The focus of proponents was on establishment of a system of ironclad guarantees that the "no strings" revenue sharing funds would be forthcoming through thick or thin; little or no attention was being given to any guarantees for the existing grant-in-aid programs. As the opponents of revenue sharing saw it, therefore, the entire scheme had to be accepted on faith, faith that not only would on-going programs be continued, but that these programs would also receive increased funds. Their opposition stemmed from an unwillingness to see the future of thirty years of policy making depend on unsecured promises coming primarily from persons who had consistently opposed adoption of these policies. Secondly, it was very evident from the new bills that revenue sharing was no longer to be considered a federal-state scheme; the local governments had to be structured into any revenue sharing bill that had any hope of getting through Congress.

But the friction between the governors and the mayors was not at an end. An immediate source of conflict, illustrating the mutual wariness over tax sharing, was the Omnibus Crime Control and Safe Streets Act of 1968, which had established the system of block grants to the states to combat crime.[9] In passing the act, Congress had provided that most of the money would go to the states, which in turn would set up planning and administrative agencies and decide how the funds would be distributed locally. Congress had mandated that at least 40 percent of the planning funds go to local governments, but it was left to the states to decide the formula for distributing the money. The cities were complaining that the states were using per capita distribution formulas, ignoring the concentration of crime in urban areas. Distribution on a per capita basis meant a small village would receive some of the money even though it might not have any crime problems; a major city might receive less than 10 percent of the money, but have 25 percent of the major crimes in the state. The mayors were saying that if the states were given control of the money, they would distribute it more for political purposes than with regard for the proportionate need of such funds in urban areas. The unhappiness of the mayors was countered by the satisfaction of the governors. At the Midwest

Governors Conference at the end of June, eleven governors from the nation's midsection expressed the view that the block grants in the crime program should serve eventually as the model for distributing other federal aid to the states.

What frightened the mayors was the continuing prospect that the governors were going to have their way. In late April, the House of Representatives, in another extension of the Elementary and Secondary Education Act, had adopted an amendment to consolidate more of the programs into a single block grant to the states. The amendment, as in 1967 proposed on the floor rather than in committee, was adopted 235 to 184, the voting showing the same lineup for block grants that had existed two years earlier, a coalition of Republicans and Southern Democrats against Northern Democrats. What had been apparent in the 90th Congress was once more made clear—if opponents of block grants and revenue sharing were to have any chance of heading off such legislation, the stand had to be made in committee. Proponents of such legislation held sway on the floor, and they now had the additional leverage of Presidential backing with its immense resources for helping persuade the reluctant, if the need arose.

THE GOVERNORS AND THE MAYORS: AGREEMENT IS REACHED

While the mayors and governors were hassling over the crime funds and the education money, the people putting the administration's bill together were actively seeking to bring the two sides together behind a single approach to tax sharing. Three possibilities were considered for distributing any shared revenues. First, have all the money go to the states and leave it up to the state officials to decide how the money would be spent. This had long been the chief fear of local officials and was unacceptable to them. Second, create two separate funds with specified percentages to go to the states and to the local communities, for example, 40 percent of the total for direct distribution to municipalities and counties. This was unacceptable to the governors, because a substantial portion of the money would bypass the states completely and because there was no common pattern of distribution of governmental costs between state and local governments. In some states, the state government bears the cost of many local programs that are the responsibilities of communities in other states. Third, there could be a mandatory pass-through. The check would go to the state, but a portion of it would have to be distributed to the local governments according to an agreed formula. In this way, the state would be given a role in the system, and the city, town, and county officials would receive needed funds.

Agreement on the issue was reached at a July 8 meeting at the White House. The meeting was attended by representatives from the National Governors' Conference, the U.S. Conference of Mayors, the National League of Cities, the National Association of Counties, the National Legislative Conference, and the International City Management Association. Speaking for the administration were the President, Vice President Agnew, Burns, and Weidenbaum. There was little disagreement at the meeting, since much of the groundwork had been done at preliminary meetings. It was tentatively agreed that the distribution to the states would be based on a formula combining population with a state's own tax effort. A state that taxed proportionately more than other states would get more under the revenue sharing formula. The state, in turn, would calculate how much of the combined state and local general revenues was raised by local governments, and this percentage would be set aside for distribution to them. For example, if in a particular state the local governments raised 35 percent of all the general revenues raised in the state, then 35 percent of the state's share would be earmarked for the local pass-through. If a particular city raised 40 percent of all local general revenues in the state, that city would receive 40 percent of the pass-through money. Finally, the basic principle was retained that no strings would be attached on how the money could be used. With the fundamentals agreed upon, it was now up to the President to take the next step.

THE PLAN GOES TO CONGRESS

On August 8, 1969, President Nixon made a television address to the nation in which he announced his plan to share federal revenues with state and local governments. He officially sent his revenue sharing message to Congress on August 13, just before it adjourned for a three-week summer vacation. In his message the President criticized the "staggering complexity and diversity" of the many existing grant programs and cited a number of problems they raised, including the growing concentration of power in Washington.

> This proposal marks a turning point in Federal-state relations, the beginning of decentralization of governmental power, the restoration of a rightful balance between the state capitals and the national capital.[10]

Despite criticism of the existing grant structure, it was made clear by administration officials explaining the plan that the money was to be a supplement to and not a substitute for the existing grant programs.[11]

Several things were to be noted about the Presidential plan:

(1) If enacted, revenue sharing was to begin the second half of fiscal year 1971. It was to be a very modest beginning, with only one-third of one percent of the presonal income tax base to be set aside for distribution. In the first full year this would be only about $1 billion. The percentage set aside would progressively rise, until in 1976 it would be one percent of the personal income tax base and, with economic expansion, would yield about $5 billion a year for distribution.

(2) All units of general local government would be eligible—cities, counties, towns, and villages. It was estimated at the outset that the state-local distribution formula would result in

state and local governments splitting the funds 50-50, nationally averaged. (As the figures were refined, however, the local government share would have been only about 30 percent with the states receiving 70 percent of the money.) The local funds would be distributed among roughly 40,000 units of government, some of them very small. It was likely that many units would receive less than $100.

(3) The plan did not attach distribution to need, either at the state or local level. There was no special equalization allocation made for the lowest income states, a provision that had been included in a number of previous revenue sharing plans.

The reaction to the Presidential plan from governors and mayors was generally favorable, but it was also felt that the amount of money was far too little. Distribution of $1 billion to governments already spending more than $100 billion was not likely to impress state and local officials. Local officials in states where nearly all the money would go to the state government were less than enthusiastic. Nevertheless, spokesmen for state, city, and county organizations hoped for quick Congressional action to get the principle of revenue sharing established.

The Presidential plan and the support it received from both governors and mayors as a result of the compromise worked out at the White House significantly altered the coalition behind revenue sharing. For five years those liberal Congressmen opposing revenue sharing had been able to sidestep the issue. President Johnson had been cool to the idea, and bills that were introduced, principally by Republicans, had languished in the House Ways and Means Committee, presided over by Chairman Mills, who had also opposed such plans in the past.

From 1964 to 1969, liberal Congressional opponents of revenue sharing also had a somewhat paradoxical relationship with the nation's mayors, who wanted the money but feared the funds would be channeled through the states and shared the fear that revenue sharing would be established at the expense of other grant programs. So, *prior* to President Nixon's taking office, the general alignment had been the President and most liberal Congressmen against revenue sharing, with Republicans and a majority of Southern Democrats (as indicated by their support of block grants) seeking to loosen the federal controls. The governors and mayors wanted the "no strings" money but were divided on who should get it. In bringing the mayors and governors together, and by pasting over the substitute issue, Nixon had succeeded in isolating the liberal Congressmen from their traditional political allies, the big city mayors. Opponents now had to rely on the bill being kept locked up in the Ways and Means Committee. This left the opposition with some uneasiness.

Mills had been steadfast in his opposition to revenue sharing, believing that the level of government that makes the taxing decisions should also be responsible for the spending decisions. "No strings" revenue sharing would separate these two responsibilities, leaving the pains of taxing to the federal government, but turning over the joys of spending to state and local authorities. (It might be inferred that Mills was also concerned that earmarking a portion of the tax base for revenue sharing impinged upon the legislative prerogatives and the taxing powers of the Ways and Means Committee.) Despite his opposition, however, Mills was not one to take unalterable positions on legislation before his committee. Mills' shift to support of Medicare in 1965 after long opposition had demonstrated the fact that the powerful chairman was capable of modifying his stand when political pressures built up sufficiently. The flexibility of Mills was to be further illustrated when he came to back Nixon's welfare reform program after initially opposing it. Nevertheless, Mills held the strategic position, and both proponents and opponents of revenue sharing knew it.

The administration bill was not formally introduced in the House until September 24, and it was apparent from the outset that the alignment in the House of Representatives had not changed.

On the first day, four administration bills were dropped into the hopper, H.R. 13982, 13983, 13984, and 13985.[12]. The four bills carried seventy-six cosponsors, all Republican. Over the next few days, additional administration bills were introduced, but they continued to carry only GOP names. Customarily, a President will seek to have his legislation introduced by the chairman of the committee having jurisdiction over the legislation, even if the chairman is of the other party. This gives a bill more prestige than if introduced by someone less important. It was apparent from the bills going in that Mills had not changed his mind; he did not sponsor the President's bill. Equally significant was the fact that the President had not even been able to persuade the ranking Republican on the Ways and Means Committee, John Byrnes of Wisconsin, to be the major sponsor. His name did not appear, and it was quickly evident that Mills and Byrnes shared their opposition to any scheme of "no strings" revenue sharing. This forced the administration to reach down to the number two Republican on the committee, Jackson Betts of Ohio, to be the major sponsor. His name topped the list on six of the administration bills introduced. In all, eighty-nine Republicans in the House, including the GOP leadership, came to sponsor the Nixon plan in the 91st Congress; no Democratic names appeared on the Nixon bill in the House.

The GOP support of the Nixon plan in 1969 represented about half of the House Republican membership. He failed to gain the cosponsorship of a large block of conservative House Republicans who had backed the substitute approach in the previous Congress. Thus, while the substitute approach had fallen from favor, it apparently was not a dead issue with some, who felt the federal Treasury could not afford any add on program without raising taxes or eliminating existing grant programs. Some GOP members also shared the conviction against separating the pains of taxing from the pleasure of spending; that is, the level of government that levies the tax should also have the responsibility for spending the revenues. Only about one-third of the GOP representatives from the southern states joined in sponsoring the bill. Many from this group, representing states with low taxes, could hardly be enthusiastic about a plan that would distribute money under a formula linked partially to such efforts. Still others held out because they customarily avoided committing themselves so early in the legislative game before hearings were held. The known opposition of Mills and Byrnes also contributed to the reluctance of some to sponsor the bill. In sum, it was clearly *not* to be assumed that the reluctance of many GOP lawmakers to introduce the bill meant that they were opposed to the concept of revenue sharing itself.

In the Senate, the Presidential plan picked up 34 sponsors, including 32 Republicans, headed by Senator Baker, and two Democrats, Sam Ervin of North Carolina and James Allen of Alabama.[13] It was clear in both House and Senate that Nixon was going to get little aid and comfort from the other side of the political aisle. The few Senate Democrats who had come to embrace revenue sharing, such as Muskie, were not going to be sucked into the policy vortex of Nixon, particularly since Muskie was already being discussed as his party's Presidential candidate for 1972.

The cumulative effect of Nixon's policy leadership was to alter the context of the revenue sharing controversy. The issue had gained visibility five years earlier when it was put forth by Heller as a fiscal transfer device geared to anticipated revenue surpluses. The political line of conflict at that time was chiefly a philosophical cleavage about the role of the national government in the federal system. But by 1969, tax sharing was becoming an increasingly partisan controversy, immersed in Congressional and Presidential politics, with the President and his fellow Republicans coming through as the most visible means of support for tax sharing.

Pushing the Old; Preparing the New

With initial policy formulation over, Presidential speech-making concluded, and the flurry of introducing bills at an end, revenue sharing was again plunged into the legislative process. In the Senate, Muskie held an intermittent series of hearings on his own bill that provided administration officials an opportunity to air the case for their version. But these hearings had more publicity than substantive value for the legislative prospects of tax sharing. In the House, tax sharing was once more locked up in the Ways and Means Committee.

Despite the inaction in Congress there was considerable activity by a number of Administration officials, including the Vice President, Weidenbaum, and Nathan. Weidenbaum and his deputy, Robert Joss, were particularly active, devoting a major part of their time to meeting with governors, mayors, state and local legislative leaders, and other key persons to get them to put pressure on their Congressmen. The two Treasury officials also took the case for revenue sharing to the media, writing dozens of articles that appeared in a variety of journals and magazines and appearing in many radio and television interviews. It was a large scale educational process to gain the support of key officials at the state and local level and the backing of the general public.

The governors, mayors, county officials, and state legislative leaders had also become fulltime partners in the lobby for tax sharing. These groups had long been interested in the issue, but had operated primarily within their own organizational constituencies. Now, with agreement reached on a distribution formula which they helped devise, these organizations had formed a grand alliance on tax sharing. The mayors' and governors' organizations sent out a revenue sharing strategy manual to their members, urging them to put pressure on Mills for House hearings. A highlight of the lobbying effort in 1970 came during the Congressional election campaigns. The White House, looking ahead to 1971, wanted to get at least 200 House members to sponsor tax sharing, including, they hoped, at least 50 Democrats. To help carry out this legislative strategy, a letter was sent to all House candidates (incumbents and challengers) urging support for tax sharing. The letter was signed by representatives of the League of Cities, Conference of Mayors, National Association of Counties, and National Legislative Conference.[14]

Meanwhile, it had become apparent that no legislative action would be forthcoming during 1970, and top officials within the administration now began to turn their sights to putting together a new plan to send to Congress in 1971. The impetus for beginning the policy formulation process anew was the annual budget. The federal budget could not be called an inspirational document, but it is a highly political document in that it reflects the decisions of a President on how he would like to spend the federal revenues in a given year. Because of its highly political nature, the grand design of the budget policy is a matter to be decided in the highest councils of Presidential advisors. It is also a document a long time in preparation. Putting together of the federal budget to cover the fiscal year that started on July 1, 1971 (fiscal year 1972), began in the early spring of 1970, about sixteen months before the money would actually begin to be spent. Preparation of the FY 72 spending program coincided with a major reorganization within the Executive Office of the President. The major changes made in 1970 were establishment of the Office of Management and Budget (OMB), built around the nucleus of the existing Bureau of the Budget, and establishment of a Domestic Council to serve as a domestic counterpart to the National Security Council. George Shultz, Secretary of Labor, was appointed to head OMB, and John Ehrlichman, a top aide to the President, was named Director of the Domestic Council.

The Domestic Council, along with OMB, became deeply involved in formulating some of the overall budget policy, and revenue sharing became an integral part of their planning. In June

President Nixon met in Louisville, Kentucky, with governors from the Appalachian states to discuss a wide range of intergovernmental policy matters. During the meeting, Weidenbaum, who accompanied Nixon, made a presentation on tax sharing which was well received by the governors and which convinced the President and his policy planners that the issue had a great deal of fiscal and political appeal. During a series of meetings in July 1970, Ehrlichman and his assistants decided to recommend to the President that tax sharing be made a high priority item in the next budget.

In late July, Nixon held a round of budget and policy review meetings in San Clemente, California, and he decided to push revenue sharing into a top policy position for the coming year. With that decision the issue was returned to his advisors for working out the details of the new program. (The new program and its formulation will be discussed in the next chapter.) The important point to be noted was that a positive decision was made by the President in mid-1970 to give revenue sharing greater priority the following year. In terms of the making of public policy, it should be further noted that the question of policy priorities was pushed to the forefront of Presidential decision making by the budget-making process, which forces the President and his top aides to make an annual review of policy piorities.

Politics Thickens

Nineteen-seventy was also a Congressional election year. Revenue sharing legislation was not directly affected by this event, but the coming of the election did set off some new pressures that were to further alter the issue environment and contribute to some major changes in President Nixon's approach to tax sharing as the year ended.

The 1968 elections had put a Republican in the White House, but had left the Congress securely in Democratic hands. With the

1970 Congressional election just ahead, the setting was ripe for a clash between the lawmakers and the chief executive as each side sought to mold the campaign to its own advantage. One of the issues was government spending and national priorities. The political argument came down to the President's charging Congress with fiscal irresponsibility and with fostering inflation by excessively boosting program levels, and the lawmakers responding that the President was ignoring domestic social needs. During 1970 Congress and the President fought back and forth over vetoes of authorization and appropriation bills.

The conflict began in January, when the President vetoed a $19.7 billion appropriation bill for the Department of Health, Education, and Welfare and the antipoverty program. The House sustained the veto when the Democrats failed to get the necessary two-thirds vote to override the President's objections. In June a second veto came, this time on a $2.8 billion authorization measure for hospital construction. This time, however, Congress voted to override the veto with a significant number of Republicans joining the Democrats to support the program. *(Chronologically,* it was after this that the Domestic Council and the President decided to make tax sharing a policy priority the next year.) In August, Nixon again received a setback when Congress voted a second time to override a Presidential spending veto. The issue was a $4.4 billion appropriation bill for the Office of Education. Again, Congressional Republicans contributed significantly to the Democratic sponsored override. The balance was immediately restored on a fourth veto, an $18 billion appropriation bill for the Department of Housing and Urban Development, the Veterans Administration, and the space program. In this House Republicans remained loyal and the Southern Democrats split their vote, providing Nixon with the necessary votes to have this veto sustained. A fifth veto was sustained in December, after the election, involving a $9.5 billion three-year authorization for manpower training.

In the short run, Congressional Democrats came out winners, as they drew unusual support from a large number of Republicans who found it politically safer to vote for additional spending on hospitals and schools than to adhere to the Presidential line on spending limits. On some spending issues many GOP members thus found themselves in the unhappy position of going against their President in an election year. It was an unpleasant position for Republicans at both ends of Pennsylvania Avenue, but it was politically acceptable since the President was not running in 1970. However, such a party split would be much more critical should it occur in 1972, when the President would share the ballot with Congressional candidates. Also, Nixon did not want to enter the 1972 Presidential campaign facing charges, rightly or wrongly, that he was neglecting domestic problems by vetoing domestic spending programs. One way around both problems would be to get revenue sharing enacted. In this way the President could point to a major innovation in federal aid to give the states and communities both more federal money and more flexibility in spending the money to meet their priorities.

But such a grand design could not be carried out with such a modest plan as proposed in 1969. It was also clear that state and local officials, although agreed on the general approach to sharing revenues, expected that any new plan would call for much larger sums. As the year closed out, reports began circulating that Nixon was beginning to think in terms of a $10 billion start that would expand to $20 billion five years after it began.[15] With the growing fiscal difficulties in many states and communities, a tax sharing plan of such proportions would, at the minimum, turn the pressure on Congress in general and, it was hoped, on Wilbur Mills in particular.

But a revenue sharing program of such magnitude presented a very great problem, as those responsible for putting together the new plan were well aware. Where was the money to come from? Federal budget deficits were averaging over $20 billion a year, and it would be extremely difficult to sell a new $10 billion program that already had strong opposition. If a politically attractive package was to be assembled, it would have to appeal to GOP fiscal conservatives and to a major block of the Southern Democrats. One way to achieve this would be to divert funds from other programs to help pay for a new revenue sharing program, a device that would appeal to these two groups who had consistently opposed new grant programs as they came along. It would not be politically wise, however, to return openly to the substitute approach and risk losing the latest members of the tax sharing coalition, the mayors, who had been the major beneficiaries of the Great Society programs. Thus, in late 1970, as the formulation of a new revenue sharing plan was under way, the formulators confronted these factors: (1) how to make the package big enough to give it high public visibility and present it as a top priority domestic program; (2) where to get enough money without losing the two extreme partners of the needed coalition, the fiscal conservatives of Congress and the mayors; (3) development of a legislative strategy that would enhance the chances of getting revenue sharing through Congress.

CHAPTER V

New Plan;
New Controversies

With the coming of the new year and a new Congress, the Nixon administration was eager to generate public interest in the new revenue sharing plan that was being put together. The President himself fed the publicity in an early January television interview in which he said the projected program was "going far beyond anything that we have suggested to date."[1] The interest of the cities was whetted with the disclosure by Weidenbaum that local governments were going to get a bigger share of the money under the new plan.[2] The 1969 proposal would have distributed about 30 percent to local governments; the new plan was to increase the local share to about 50 percent. If all of this sounded ominous to the President's conservative backers, the balance was redressed by newspaper accounts that the administration was cutting back existing federal aid programs, including some urban assistance, to help provide money for the new plan. (This report disturbed key officials in the White House, who had been working in secrecy to put the new package together. They suspected that the report of urban aid cutbacks had been leaked by persons in the Model Cities agency who feared their own program was in jeopardy.)

The total effect was to create the image of an active administration in the final stages of assembling a major new piece of domestic legislation. What remained was the public announcement.

It had been decided that the President's State of the Union Message would be the vehicle for making the plan known to Congress and to the American people. This message is one of the three major policy presentations of the President, the other two being the annual Budget Message and the Economic Report. Of the three, the State of the Union gets the greatest public visibility. It is the one which the President personally delivers before the Congress. (Nixon broke this tradition in 1973, when he did not personally present the Message, but he reverted to a personal appearance in 1974.) It therefore is carried by the television networks in its entirety and gets the headlines in the newspapers. If the President wished to make tax sharing a major and highly visible issue, disclosing the new plan in the State of the Union would certainly help achieve this effect.

Nixon went before Congress to deliver his message on the evening of January 22. It was a rather peculiar message. The United States was still heavily involved in Vietnam and the nation remained sharply divided on the pace of American withdrawal. But the President's message did not mention Vietnam nor any other matters of foreign policy. The only mention of foreign affairs was the statement that a separate report on foreign policy would be issued the following month. Nixon had chosen to place all emphasis on domestic issues without having them compete with such contentious matters as Vietnam.

The message was unusual in another sense. State of the Union Messages have commonly been a grab bag of foreign and domestic policy statements with something for everyone, ranging across such items as housing programs, civil rights, health needs, natural resources, farm policy, defense needs, and relations with other nations. On the domestic side, they have traditionally been bureaucratic packages, in the sense that the pieces are patched together after canvassing the federal agencies during the budget process to find out what they would like to have in the way of new policies and programs during the coming year. It is a victory for those agencies and their constituents who get their wants included in the message. This is no guarantee that anything will be forthcoming by way of money or legislation, but it is a mark of Presidential blessing. In this context, Nixon's 1971 State of the Union Message was antibureaucratic in two ways. First, it focused on only three subjects—welfare reform, tax sharing, and reorganization of the federal executive branch. The only other policy proposed was a call for $100 million in federal money to help eradicate cancer. Secondly, revenue sharing and reorganization would radically alter the federal role in the making of public policy in ways that threatened to disestablish some agencies and re-organize many others.

The President's message was aimed at "opening the way to a new American revolution—a peaceful revolution in which power was turned back to the people—in which government at all levels was refreshed and renewed, and made truly responsive." The proposed welfare reforms called for a greater federal policy role in setting income standards, and the reorganization plan was aimed at rationalizing the federal bureaucracy. It was thus apparent that revenue sharing was the cornerstone of the revolution, and it was the portion of the message that got the most publicity. If headlines in *The New York Times* are any indication of the importance of news, then Nixon had eminently succeeded in raising the public profile of tax sharing. In 1969 the President's announcement of his plan got one column on page one. In 1971, the paper carried a large type, four column headline on revenue sharing.[3] By this standard revenue sharing had arrived. It could hardly have done otherwise.

What the President proposed was a $16 billion package that, by the dollar amount, made the plan of 1969 fade into insignificance. To desperate governors, mayors, city managers, and county supervisors, it was a most impressive sum that would help turn the heat on recalcitrant Congressmen. But in putting the new plan together, Nixon had greatly distorted the original principle of tax sharing. The basic concept of revenue sharing had been that the federal government pays to the states and local governments an amount of money to be used for general governmental purposes without specifying how the money would be used; that is, "no strings" is fundamental to the idea. Of equal importance is that the money will be forthcoming through thick or thin and not subject to the political needs of the President or Congress. In his new plan, however, the President presented tax sharing in a new form, or rather two forms—*general* revenue sharing and *special* revenue sharing.

The general tax sharing portion was in accord with the basic concept. Nixon proposed an initial sum of $5 billion a year in new money for general support. The biggest change from the 1969 bill was in the amount of money. The larger sum was provided primarily by increasing the percentage of the shared revenues to .96 percent of the personal income tax base the first year and 1.3 percent in succeeding years. Another change made was in the local distribution formula which, on a national average, would allot local governments about half of the money. Every county, city, and town would be eligible for funds without regard to population size. The Nixon plan of 1971 was, in its total effect, more favorable toward local governments than the 1969 plan had been. The mayors had been rewarded for their support.

Special revenue sharing, on the other hand, introduced new elements into the controversy. The President proposed taking $10 billion from existing grant programs plus $1 billion in new money. The total of $11 billion would go for grants in six broad areas—urban development, rural development, education, transportation, job training, and law enforcement. Nixon did not give any details in his speech about these funds, but the individual plans subsequently submitted to Congress showed that they would range from $500 million a year for law enforcement to approximately $3 billion for education. Other important features were that special revenue sharing would eliminate all matching fund requirements and the funds would be distributed automatically without the need of prior federal approval of applications or plans.

Despite the title "special revenue sharing," what Nixon actually did was to propose establishment of six block grants to be funded mainly from existing categorical aid funds. The provision for automatic distribution of the funds differed from previous block grant programs calling for prior federal approval of state plans, but this did not make the new program "revenue sharing." By calling this "special revenue sharing," he was able to present the appearance of a massive new tax sharing program which, in fact, was two-thirds funded from old programs. In the process he had undermined the basic revenue sharing concept in that the special programs attached broad conditions to their use. And, as the actual special revenue sharing bills were drawn up, the conditions increased, particularly in education special revenue sharing, which came to be further subdivided on the kinds of education programs that could receive the funds. The special funds also departed from revenue sharing in that each fund, once established, would have to go through the regular budget and appropriation steps, an uncertain process that provides no assurances about the amount of money to be provided.

The manipulation of the term revenue sharing did not go over well with some of the advocates of tax sharing. Senator Baker, Nixon's chief revenue sharing sponsor in the Senate, told a Senate hearing in late spring about his own unhappiness with the concept of special revenue sharing. "I have always been a little bit concerned that the administration chose to call this program in this respect special revenue sharing; it is in no way revenue sharing," he said.[4]

The issue was not just a semantical one. Special revenue sharing, in proposing the elimination of many separate categorical programs, would do precisely what many lawmakers had long feared. It would eliminate many of the federal policy controls and turn the money over to state and local officials, leaving them to make the important decisions on what programs would actually be funded. In the past, general revenue sharing had posed only a potential threat to the categorical grants. Special revenue sharing represented a direct and immediate threat. Also, the elimination of the matching grant requirements held the possibility of a reduction in the total amount being spent in the special areas. The President proposed adding $1 billion in new money to the six special programs, but with the elimination of matching requirements the required commitment at the state and local would be reduced by about $3 billion. Unless state and local governments went ahead with their own spending, the net effect could be $2 billion less spent in the six areas.

Before looking at the development of the controversy after the State of the Union address, it is necessary to take a look at how the 1971 package had been formulated and how the concept of special revenue sharing had evolved. The formulation process for the 1971 plan also reveals the attachment of the President to the concept of using revenue sharing as a substitute for grant-in-aid programs, an issue that supposedly expired in 1969.

POLICY FORMULATION:
THE PRESIDENT AND HIS STAFF

In July 1970, Nixon had decided to make tax sharing a major policy proposal for 1971, but few specifics had been worked out in the immediate months following. Work began in earnest in the late fall. Two days after the November Congressional elections Nixon asked his staff to consider the possibility of vastly expanding the tax sharing program by *eliminating all* categorical grants and using the funds for revenue sharing. The President told his staff that during his campaign trips he had detected a growing frustration among the American people, who felt that government had become unresponsive to their needs. The people wanted the government brought closer to them so they could make it respond to their wishes. Converting categorical grant money into revenue sharing would help achieve this, he said.[5]

The responsibility of working out the details was given to Ehrlichman and his Domestic Council staff. The job was turned over to two of Ehrlichman's top assistants—Edwin Harper and Edward Morgan. Morgan had the day-to-day responsibility for the program while Harper was more concerned with theoretical and intellectual questions. The Office of Management and Budget was also intimately involved, and Nathan and others from OMB started to prepare a list of all categorical grant programs, with the idea of transforming them into a revenue sharing fund of $30 billion a year. (This was the approximate amount that was being spent annually on grant programs.) The idea of phasing out all grant programs did not last long. It was quickly seen that there were many mechanical and political problems that would make a total conversion very difficult. Now a Presidential decision was needed on how far to go on eliminating categorical grants. That decision was made during the President's trip to Europe to attend the funeral of French President Charles De Gaulle in the second week of November. Nixon was accompanied by members of his staff, who discussed with him the idea of a complete phaseout of grants. The President decided he would not seek a total conversion and returned the problem to his staff, asking them to prepare a proposal on which programs should be retained and which should be phased into revenue sharing. The practical result was the division of revenue sharing into the two categories—general and special.

There emerged two centers of gravity for formulating the new plan. Weidenbaum and the Treasury Department remained the focal point for developing what came to be general revenue sharing. Weidenbaum continued his liaison with state and local lobbyists, and he had the responsibility for revising the distribution formula to increase the local share from 30 percent to approximately 50 percent. Ehrlichman and the Domestic Council staff had the job of formulating the special revenue sharing portion of the plan. Treasury, the Domestic Council staff, and OMB staff members stayed in communication on overall progress, but their responsibilities were clearly distinct.

The division of responsibilities for preparing the two parts carried with it significant differences in how the jobs were done. Weidenbaum and those working on general revenue sharing did much of their work in the open, making speeches, holding meetings, and maintaining communications with state and local lobbying organizations. It was an open system of policy formulation. The basic outlines of tax sharing were already known, and what changes were being made in the proposal were essentially incremental changes having to do with distribution formulas and the percentage of money to be shared. On these matters state and local lobbyists had already been deeply involved and this practice continued. The only major piece of information not revealed to these groups was the amount of money contemplated in the new policy.

The openness of this portion of the policy formulation was demonstrated by a meeting held in Atlanta, Georgia, in December 1970, where Weidenbaum met with officials of eight state and local organizations to discuss many of the details of the new plan, including a revised distribution formula to increase the local share of the money. The meeting, arranged by the National League of Cities, also included representatives from the National Governors' Conference, National Legislative Conference, National Association of Counties, National Conference of State Legislative Leaders, National Society of State Legislators, U.S. Conference of Mayors, and the International City Management Association.

The formulation of special revenue sharing was, on the other hand, a much more secretive process throughout, and the closer Ehrlichman and his staff got to ironing out the details of the new plan the more closed the formulation process became. The secrecy stemmed from a desire to heighten the public and political impact of the new policy when it was announced by the President. There was little chance of keeping the new program secret if persons outside of the President's closest advisors became aware of the details of the plan being developed. It was evident also that special revenue sharing would not sit well with many Congressmen, interest groups, and bureaucratic agencies. Many of these had an interest in programs being considered for liquidation, and it was probable that they would start political backfires if they became aware of the specifics of what was being developed within the White House.

By late November the Domestic Council staff and OMB had worked out the tentative estimates of the amounts available from categorical grants. It was once more time to clear the progress with the President so work could proceed on details. On December 12, a presentation on revenue sharing was made to Nixon as part of a meeting on the new budget being prepared. Attending the meeting were Nixon, Ehrlichman, Shultz, OMB Deputy Director Caspar Weinberger, Harper, and Paul McCracken, Chairman of the Council of Economic Advisers. At this meeting Nixon gave his approval to the staff work and also said that other persons could be informed of the pro and con arguments of converting categorical grants into revenue sharing. However, details about specific programs and the amount of money involved were kept secret.

In early January Nixon began to make some of the final key decisions about the new revenue sharing program. The budget was in the final stages of preparation and the dollar figures for revenue sharing had to be included in the President's spending plan. On January 3, in San Clemente, Nixon decided to go ahead with the $5 billion general revenue sharing and six special revenue sharing programs totaling $11 billion. At this point, no final determination had been made on the list of grant programs that would be converted into special revenue sharing.

On January 12, Nixon made the final decision. It was a carefully guarded secret. Only those with an imperative need to know were told of the decision on general and special revenue sharing. The actual dollar figures and programs involved were even more closely guarded. It was not until January 19 that the President's Cabinet was called in to be informed by Weidenbaum of the tax sharing contents of the State of the Union address to be delivered three days later.

There are several things to be noted about the formulation of Nixon's 1971 tax sharing plan. One is that the formulation process, particularly the special tax sharing portion, was centered in Nixon's closest and most trusted advisers. Congressmen were not privy to the details of the program, and the bureaucracy, the source of much policy formulation, was deliberately kept out. Lobbying organizations were involved in revising the distribution formula of general revenue sharing, but were not participants in designing the special tax sharing program.

A second point was the key role played by the Domestic Council. The Council had just been created, and one of the first assignments of the Council staff, headed by Ehrlichman, had been the responsibility for formulating a major new domestic policy for the President. The influence of the Council staff on the policy process was thus quickly established, and it became a center for long-range domestic policy planning for Nixon.* The Council was not,

*The Domestic Council must be distinguished from the Council staff. The Council itself, as initially established, was made up of the President, Vice President, cabinet secretaries in charge of domestic programs, and a number of Presidential aides. This group seldom met and rarely made decisions. The Council staff, headed by an Executive Director, was the real source of Council influence. The staff was responsible for much of the domestic policy formulation and, through the Executive Director, was in frequent contact with the President. With the Watergate scandal and the departure of John Ehrlichman from the White House, the influence of the Council staff declined and its future relations with the President and its role in domestic policy planning are uncertain.

however, the only Executive Office influence on the President in the area of domestic policy. The Office of Management and Budget has the basic responsibility for monitoring the day-to-day operations of the government and for preparing the budget. As seen in the preparation of special revenue sharing, OMB was the locus of much expertise and detailed information needed by the Council staff to carry out its policy-planning function.

Finally, the role of the President in the formulation of revenue sharing policy is instructive about Presidential decision making. The President has many demands on his time and has little opportunity to involve himself personally in any continuous way in the development of long-range policy. This is the responsibility of his staff. Presidents do not have time to contemplate policies or programs in the abstract. They act in concrete situations that are brought before them. In the case of tax sharing, though Nixon provided the original suggestion, set guidelines, and made the key decisions, he personally entered the formulation process only when it was necessary for the most important decisions to be made, and these decisions were timed to meet budget and message schedules.

MOBILIZING POLITICAL PRESSURE: MILLS AGREES TO HEARINGS, BUT . . .

The Nixon administration had solved the problem of raising the visibility of revenue sharing by putting together a $16 billion package. What now faced White House staffers was development of a legislative strategy that would get the bill through Congress. Some of the groundwork had already been laid during the previous fall by the lobbying campaign among all Congressional candidates. Now, however, the dimensions of the new plan were known and specific commitments had to be secured. The overall strategy was to put pressure on the Congress to act, and this meant that Chairman Mills had to be nudged from his long-held position of killing revenue sharing by ignoring it.

Mills' legislative power was not only due to the fact that he was Chairman of the Ways and Means Committee (and thus also Chairman of the Democratic Committee on Committees), but also because he had the reputation for being most careful in doing his legislative homework and for being sensitive to the wishes of his committee members. He would not stand in the way of legislation he personally opposed if it was clear that a majority of his committee and the House as a whole wanted it. In such situations, rather than folding under the pressure, he sought to tailor the legislation more to his own views. White House political strategists were aware of Mills' *modus operandi,* and so geared their tactics to pressuring him into a more flexible position.

It was anticipated that the necessary pressure would come from several directions. First, state and local lobbyists had long been urging Mills to at least allow revenue sharing a hearing in his committee. Second, it was hoped that the new bill to be introduced would be cosponsored by 200 or more House members, including 50 or 60 Democrats. This would serve as a signal to Mills that revenue sharing had broad based, bipartisan support in the House. Third, pressure was to be generated within Mills' own committee. Throughout the time the issue was before the Ways and Means Committee considerable contact work with members of the Committee was carried on by the Treasury Department through James Smith, head of the Department's legislative liaison. The responsibility for orchestrating these Congressional pressures went to the White House Congressional Relations Office, headed by former Representative Clark MacGregor.

Intensive lobbying of Capitol Hill began on the same day as Nixon's speech. On January 22, Nixon met with Representative Byrnes, ranking Republican on the Ways and Means Committee. Byrnes had declined to sponsor the President's first revenue sharing bill in 1969, but there was hope that the Wisconsin lawmaker could be persuaded to be the major sponsor in 1971 or at least not to help Mills to block hearings. The administration also launched a series of briefings for key Congressmen on its revenue sharing plan. The immediate post-Message lobbying was capped by inviting all members of Congress to the White House for breakfast briefings on tax sharing and government reorganization. It was a large scale educational-legislative lobbying effort to get a majority of Congressmen to support the bill, followed by smaller sessions with Committee and other key members of Congress.[6]

On January 24 Nixon got support from the Gallup Poll, which reported that 77 percent of a poll were in favor of tax sharing while only 14 percent opposed. Nine percent had no opinion. Support came from the ranks of Democrats, Republicans, and Independents.

The next day the first major hurdle to revenue sharing toppled when Mills and Byrnes said they would allow a Congressional hearing on the plan. But Mills, after a private meeting with the President, added a greater qualifier. He said he would hold hearings, "But not for the purpose of promoting the plan—for the purpose of killing it."[7] Mills' concession on hearings was what the White House political strategists had hoped for. They reasoned that sufficient pressure could be built up so the Chairman would agree to some kind of legislation getting out of his committee.

Having announced that hearings would be held, Mills now took the offensive against the administration plan. In the past he had said repeatedly that he opposed any tax sharing scheme, his opposition based on arguments about the responsibilities of Congress to assure that tax monies are spent properly and on the unavailability of revenues to share. Now, however, this was no longer a sufficient counterargument. The issue had become too visible and too political to be handled on a general level. If the administration sought friends with arguments of how much tax sharing would mean to their areas, any counterattack would have to make the point that not everyone gains. This was the approach that Mills took.

On January 26, just four days after the Nixon speech, Mills made a major speech in the House listing defects he found in the plan and offering a variety of alternatives to tax sharing.[8] His speech and answers to questions lasted more than an hour—long for the House—and drew more attendance than usual for a matter not directly related to a bill under consideration. He confined his remarks to general revenue sharing.

He made these major points:

(1) He acknowledged that a significant number of urban areas had serious fiscal problems and that answers must be found. The proliferation of federal grants had contributed to this problem, but the root cause of the difficulties was increasing urbanism and the complexities this brought.

(2) He made two assumptions. If revenue sharing were adopted it would mean either a cutback on other expenditures, or more spending to be financed through increased taxes. He said he personally would choose reduced expenditures if tax sharing were adopted.

(3) If expenditures were reduced, whether in all areas or just in grant programs to finance tax sharing, about a third of the states (which he listed) would actually lose federal money. The losers would include some of the states with the greatest welfare problems and with relatively low per capita income. In other words, the money would not go where it was needed most.

(4) If revenue sharing was financed from increased taxes, the wealthier states would pay more in taxes than they would receive from revenue sharing.

In his speech Mills also presented possible alternatives to tax sharing to help states and cities deal with their problems. They were:

(1) Let the states adopt income tax laws setting their taxes as a percentage of the federal tax. The federal government would collect the taxes, turn the revenues over to the states, and bear the administrative costs.

(2) Establish a tax credit system to allow taxpayers to credit part

of their state income tax against their federal tax. This would permit states to raise their taxes.

(3) Consolidate some of the categorical grants into broader block grants to simplify the grant system.

(4) Increase the federal share of some of the existing grant programs. This would reduce the state and local matching share and free that money for other purposes. This approach could be applied to areas of education, welfare, hospitals, and health, which accounted for nearly 60 percent of state and local government expenditures.

The effect of Mills' speech was to alert some Congressmen that revenue sharing could actually cost their constituents money. The Chairman's speech thus raised the sensitive points of potential fiscal losses and/or possible tax increases, a set of conditions designed to discourage members from sponsoring the Nixon bill and to arm them with reasons for holding out. In presenting alternatives, Mills also provided his fellow legislators with some positive approaches to dealing with state and local fiscal problems. All of this served as Mills' counterpressure to administration efforts to get as many legislative cosponsors as possible.

For submittal to Congress, the administration divided the plan into seven pieces. This was done partly at the urging of the state and local organizations, who did not wish to jeopardize the prospects for general revenue sharing by having it tied to the even more contentious special revenue sharing, and partly because Treasury officials also urged the White House to divide the package to avoid the problem of committee jurisdiction. The biggest piece was general revenue sharing, which went to Congress on February 4. Nothing was forthcoming from the White House at that time on legislation for special revenue sharing. In sending his general sharing plan to Congress, Nixon said only that the $11 billion special program would be spelled out "in a series of subsequent messages." It was clear there was no close connection between general and special revenue sharing.

Meanwhile, the general revenue sharing bill was introduced in Congress. Mills and other opponents of Nixon's program won the first round. The number of House sponsors fell far short of what the White House had sought. The administration bills were H.R. 4187-4193. Nixon had hoped for at least 200 House sponsors; he got 139. This was a large number, but was about a third less than the goal. The number of Democrats joining was even more disappointing. White House lobbyists were seeking 50 to 60 Democratic cosponsors; they got just eight.

The Senate bill, S. 680, was sponsored by Baker and 36 fellow Senators. The list included 33 Republicans and four Democrats. It was clear in both the House and the Senate that the issue, at least in terms of who was introducing and cosponsoring the President's plan, was becoming increasingly divided along partisan lines. The politicization of revenue sharing was even more apparent from the results of the administration's efforts to recruit Muskie as a cosponsor. Weidenbaum, representatives of city and county groups, and Baker talked with members of Muskie's staff and with Muskie himself about sponsoring the Nixon bill. Muskie declined.[9]

Congress Wary on Special Revenue Sharing

The special revenue sharing plans began to arrive on Capitol Hill on March 2 with the President's message on law enforcement revenue sharing. The last of the six special programs, education, went to Congress on April 6. The messages were stretched out partly to achieve maximum publicity value for tax sharing and partly to give the bill drafters time to iron out problems. When the bills were referred to committees, it was clear how fragmented revenue sharing had become. In all, the $16 billion plan had been divided up among eleven different Congressional committees.

The White House did not conduct a major campaign for sponsors of special revenue sharing bills comparable to the effort on general tax sharing, and it was quickly apparent that Congress was being very cautious about this part of Nixon's new policy. The attitude of Congress could be described as frigid on the part of Democratic lawmakers and cautiously cool on the part of Republicans. There were two basic reasons for this reception.

First, there was the belief that special revenue sharing would result in the liquidation or shrinkage of ongoing programs. That is, special revenue sharing threatened many policy subsystems and would have terminated or disrupted the multitude of complex, vested relationships that had grown up between Congressional committees, bureaucrats, and interest groups. Special sharing did not eliminate any programs *per se*, but it did end their federal sponsorship. If a local government wished to continue a particular program with special revenue sharing funds, it could do so. If it wished to end the program or cut its funding, it could do that also without any loss of other funds. The Congressional backers of the programs marked for liquidation feared the latter would frequently happen, with the money then going for other purposes such as

TABLE III

Congressional Committee Jurisdiction
over Revenue Sharing Bills

Name	House Committee	H.R. Bill #	Senate Committee	S. Bill #
General R.S.	Ways and Means	4187	Finance	680
Law Enforcement	Judiciary	5408	Judiciary	1087
Manpower	Education and Labor	6181	Labor-Public Welfare	1243
Urban Development	Banking and Currency	8853	Banking-Housing-Urban	1618
Rural Development	Government Operations	7993	Agriculture	1612
Transportation	Ways and Means	13021	Commerce	1693
Education	Education and Labor	7796	Labor-Public Welfare	1669

pay raises for big municipal worker unions. There was also the concern that the money would be used to allow a reduction in local property taxes. This, along with dropping the matching fund requirements, could result in a reduction or leveling off of fiscal commitments to solving difficult social and economic problems. Many also did not like the idea of automatic distribution of the money without prior federal approval. Automatic distribution of the money under a formula meant that some communities would share in the special funds which had never participated in the categorical grant programs to be eliminated. For example, urban renewal funds were to become part of the urban development special fund. Some cities that never had an urban renewal project would get part of that money and cities that were active in urban renewal would have to scale down or eliminate new projects.

The second reason for Congressional caution was linked to the sources and distribution of power in Congress. Congressional power is decentralized, with the committees and subcommittees as the principal loci. Within these committees and subcommittees power is further distributed on the basis of seniority. Congress can be viewed as a multitude of pyramids, representing the committee and subcommittee hierarchies. The House leadership—the Speaker, party floor leaders, and party whips—act as influential party brokers in this system of decentralized power.

The source of a committee's power is its jurisdiction over a particular area of public policy. Committees are not of equal importance. The House Appropriations Committee with its power of the purse casts a larger shadow than the House Committee on Merchant Marine and Fisheries; the Armed Services Committee with its links to the Pentagon does more important things than the House Administration Committee. While this is true in general, it is not true in particular policy areas. School teachers and administrators are more interested in what is going on in the Education and Labor Committee than in the Judiciary Committee; a Model Cities administrator in Boston is more concerned with the Banking and Currency Committee, which handles that program, than he is in the Armed Services business. By their jurisdiction over particular policies, the committees are also very influential with the bureaucracies administering the programs. Defense Department officials are responsive to the Chairman of the Armed Services Committee and *vice versa;* Office of Education officials care most about the views of the committees having jurisdiction over their programs.

These policy linkages are also mutual, in that the legislative committees expect support from their bureaucratic and interest group partners in maintaining and expanding programs in which they have a mutual interest. A committee's pyramid is enlarged by its having authority over growing programs; its pyramid shrinks if it finds its programs dwindling or disappearing. Special revenue sharing loomed as a threat to this system of mutual accommodation and reliance. The President was proposing that many particular programs be joined into six special purpose funds which would be automatically distributed. For example, the Urban Community Development Revenue Sharing Act proposed that the $2 billion plan be funded in part by elimination of the Model Cities grants as a separate, federally sponsored program. This loomed as a threat to local Model Cities officials, who would have to rely for survival on the discretion of local government. In Congress, to some committee members, it meant limitations on their influence over the content of policy and the direction of spending.

Over and above this system of committee "interests" is a general Congressional chariness about raids into these committee fiefdoms. The rules of the game frown on efforts from any source to limit or remove a committee's prerogatives. When invasions do occur, such as trimming the authority of the Rules Committee to block legislation from going to the floor, it disrupts Congressional behavioral norms and leaves behind pockets of disharmony in an institution that takes pride in harmony and mutual accommodation. Therefore, there are few occasions when it is considered necessary or wise to interfere with committee operations. (In the spring of 1974, House Democrats declined to approve a major proposal to revise the House committee structure and realign committee jurisdictions. It would have been the first major reorganization of House committees since 1946.)

Connected with this is the touchy matter of committee jurisdiction. For example, Rural Development Revenue Sharing contemplated consolidating programs some of which had been under the jurisdiction of the Agriculture Committee, and some under the Public Works Committee. Which committee should it go to? Transportation revenue sharing involved highway, mass transit, and airport programs which came under the jurisdiction of four different House committees: establishment of the highway programs was done with legislation from the Public Works Committee while the Highway Trust Fund was the work of both the Public Works and Ways and Means Committees; mass transit programs were authorized by the Banking and Currency Committee; airport building programs were the province of the Interstate and Foreign Commerce Committee.

Clearly, Nixon's special revenue sharing plans, with their implicit repercussions on committee jurisdiction and Congressional behavioral norms, were not considered vital enough, at the early stage of bill introduction, to force members to flock to their support. The result was that the individual special tax sharing bills drew very little open backing when they were introduced.*

THE REVENUE SHARING LOBBY

Revenue sharing was not an issue that could sell itself. Despite the big public support given it as indicated by the polls, it was, in fact, an issue without emotional appeal or deeply held conviction

*None of the special revenue sharing plans was enacted during the 92nd Congress. Unless otherwise specified, the subsequent material in this volume is concerned only with general revenue sharing.

as far as the mass of the public was concerned. Most people probably had never heard of tax sharing or if they did, they had only the vaguest notion of what it was all about. The real constituency for revenue sharing was the nation's governors, state legislators, and local leaders. Therefore, if Congress was to be pressured into action, it would not be by any national Presidential appeals on television or popular barnstorming, but by selling the idea to the key state and local leaders and to their lobbying organizations. Counter pressure would be difficult. Governors, legislators, and local leaders needed money and were not likely to be receptive to views opposing tax sharing. What organized opposition to revenue sharing did exist was composed of strange political bedfellows—the AFL-CIO, the U.S. Chamber of Commerce, the American Farm Bureau Federation, and the National Association of Manufacturing—who were only indirectly affected by tax sharing. The AFL-CIO opposition was based on the belief that revenue sharing would mean the termination of many categorical programs which it supported, while the Chamber, Farm Bureau, and NAM saw revenue sharing necessitating a tax increase. They did not have the same standing as elected state and local officials, who directly felt the pressure of fiscal problems. If lobbying effectiveness is related to intensity of feeling on an issue, it was clear that the pro-revenue sharing group had more leverage.

The first round of the dispute had gone to Mills and opponents of revenue sharing by keeping the number of sponsors down. Now the administration, led by President Nixon and Vice President Agnew, became actively engaged in selling the plan to state and local officials. This selling campaign outside of Washington was part of the overall strategy to create a national pro-revenue sharing political environment that Mills and the Congress could not ignore.

President Nixon himself made a plea for his plan in early March in a speech in Des Moines, Iowa; and following a meeting between

Nixon and four midwestern governors there, Democratic Governor Warren E. Hearnes of Missouri announced he was switching to support of revenue sharing. Agnew was assigned the role of top salesman for the revenue sharing package and soon after the bills were introduced, he set out on a major promotion tour that took him from New York City to Hilo, Hawaii. The many stops were well staged, with the Vice President frequently going before a well publicized meeting of the state legislature or a large statewide group of officials. Such meetings were usually followed by private conferences with the Governor and other key state leaders. While Agnew was traveling around selling tax sharing, Chairman Mills was embarked on a more modest counteroperation, also with state legislators. For example, in early May, Agnew made an appeal for support before a joint session of the Tennessee legislature. Six days later Mills went to Tennessee to make the opposite appeal.

Special attention was given to the mayors, who, it was felt, were the key to pressuring Mills and other Congressional opponents. On March 22 Agnew and George Romney, Secretary of Housing and Urban Development, went before a meeting of representatives of the National League of Cities and the U.S. Conference of Mayors. By this time the administration presentation was well known and standardized. What surprised the mayors, however, was a speech to them the same day by Senator Muskie, then a leading contender to be the Democratic opponent of Nixon the following year. Muskie, who had become a leading Democratic advocate of tax sharing, urged the mayors to oppose the Nixon plan, and he suggested that a federal takeover of welfare would have greater financial benefits than tax sharing. Muskie's speech had strong overtones of Presidential politics and his unexpected change of views angered the mayors, who, after early wariness about the scheme, were now solid members of the pro-revenue sharing coalition and had become the most active lobbyists for the program. Before leaving town, thirty of the mayors met almost two hours with Nixon and went away with a friendly attitude toward the Republican President and critical of their usual friends, the Democrats in Congress. The mayors were particularly upset with Muskie. The Senator, to show he was not abandoning revenue sharing, but only suggesting a politically acceptable alternative, soon introduced a new sharing bill of his own which favored the larger cities.

It was evident that no serious candidate for the office of President could be opposed to revenue sharing, and it became a necessary part of the campaign baggage that each have his own plan. To vacillate on this issue was to incur the wrath of the state and local leaders, particularly the nation's mayors. Senator Humphrey, who returned to the Senate in January, had his plan, which he co-sponsored with Representative Henry Reuss; Senator George McGovern, who had never shown much interest in tax sharing, now had a proposal; and the subsequent conversion of Mills, who later entered the Presidential race, was indicative of the political potency of the issue.

Alternative Plans

By the spring of 1971, it was apparent that tax sharing now had some momentum. The previous barrier, the House Ways and Means Committee, had been breached with Mills' concession to hold hearings, even if to kill the bill. At this point, it would be useful to examine briefly the major alternative bills being proposed for general revenue sharing and the alternatives to revenue sharing itself that were being offered.

(1) *Nixon plan* (H.R. 4187). The President's plan proposed to set aside 1.3 percent of the personal income tax base to be returned to state and local governments to use as they saw fit.* The funds

---

*The income tax base (net taxable income after deductions) was used rather than income tax revenues, because the former varies primarily with the national economy, generally an upward growth, while tax revenues are subject to fluctuations with changes both in the national economy and tax rates. It was thought desirable to avoid uncertainty over the amount of revenue sharing funds that could result from upward or downward adjustments in the personal income tax rate.

would be split about evenly between the states and local governments. At the start, about $5 billion a year would be made available, rising in subsequent years as the economy and tax base expanded. The funds were to be distributed among the states by a formula based on population, with an adjustment for "tax effort" to reward those states making a greater effort to meet their needs from their own resources. Within the states the money would be distributed to every town, city, and county, with the share of each determined by the ratio that its tax collections bore to the total local revenues raised within the state.

(2) *Muskie bill* (S. 1770). This plan, like the Nixon bill, proposed setting aside 1.3 percent of the taxable personal income base. *In addition*, Muskie proposed that federal funds equal to 10 percent of the total amount of income taxes collected by state governments be returned on a proportional basis to states with income taxes. This additional 10 percent bonus was intended as a reward for states with income taxes and as an incentive for states without such taxes to adopt them. The bonus would also encourage a state with a narrow income tax base to expand it. The bonus money would mean an additional $1 billion for distribution, raising the total amount of the general revenue sharing fund to $6 billion annually to start.

Another major difference between the Muskie bill and the Nixon plan was that the former authorized only a five-year program. Muskie's view was that this provided a long enough period for state and local governments to make firm plans for use of the money, but also guaranteed a Congressional review of the tax sharing program after it had been in effect for a reasonable period of time.

A third major difference was that the Muskie bill established a different distribution formula, based on need as well as population and tax effort. Generally, the need factor was dependent on concentrations of poor persons. In introducing the need factor, the Muskie bill also weighted the distributions in favor of larger cities, counties, and townships, where low income residents had concentrated.

An added feature of the Muskie bill was that it permitted, as a matter of convenience to the states, the federal government to collect state income taxes. This was aimed at simplifying tax filing for the individual and cutting the states' administrative costs for tax collection.

(3) *Humphrey-Reuss bill* (S. 241). This proposal was distinct in several fundamental ways from either the Nixon or the Muskie bill. First, the funding provisions were not tied to the federal income tax, and thus the bill was far removed from the basic concepts of revenue sharing even though the sponsors called it that. It was in fact a block grant bill that would provide $3 billion the first year; $5 billion the second, $7 billion the third, and $9 billion the fourth. It was a four-year program only, and, more importantly, the appropriation was not automatic each year, but would have to go through the regular, and hazardous, budgeting and Congressional appropriation process. Thus there was no assurance that all of the money would be forthcoming.

A further distinction was that the funds were tied to a state's willingness to modernize and streamline its governmental systems and processes, rather than being given with no strings. To qualify for funds after the first year, a state had to prepare a master plan and timetable for modernizing state and local government. Among the reforms suggested was adoption or widening the base of state income taxes. The Humphrey-Reuss bill thus carried a significant string, governmental modernization, on distribution of the funds. The case for modernization could easily be made in many states, but such an approach was anathema to the many state and local beneficiaries of antiquated governmental structures and processes.

The percentage of funds passed through to local governments would vary among the states, ranging from 30 to 65 percent. The bill also encouraged concentration of money in the larger cities and towns where it was most needed.

(4) *Tax credits.* Since tax sharing was revitalized as an issue in 1964, many persons had suggested the use of tax credits as an

alternative means of helping state and local governments out of their financial difficulties. Among the proponents of tax credits was Representative John Byrnes, ranking Republican on the Ways and Means Committee.

The tax credit concept was not new. It was originally employed to avoid double taxation, so that Americans paying taxes to foreign governments on income earned abroad would not have to pay a tax on the same money in the United States. The American taxpayer was allowed to take a credit for the taxes paid to the foreign government against taxes he would otherwise pay to the United States. The states use income tax credit in a similar fashion, so a taxpayer does not have to pay a tax on the same income in two states.

As an alternative to revenue sharing, a tax credit basically would mean that a portion (for example, 40 percent) of state income taxes paid could be taken as a credit against the federal income tax liability. This would mean reduced tax collections by the federal government, but provide an opportunity to the states to levy or raise their own income taxes without increasing the taxpayers' total tax bill. The tax credit would not provide any automatic income to the state; it would give the states an opportunity to increase their collections if they were willing to levy or raise their own taxes. It therefore required an act of political courage by state governors and legislators and was not enthusiastically embraced as an alternative to tax sharing by these groups.

A tax credit would help states without income taxes to levy them, and it would help those with a low rate to increase them. But those states with relatively high income taxes, such as New York, would find the federal tax credit of less assistance. Another drawback to the tax credit alternative was that it channeled about 90 percent of the aid to the states, local government having few income tax levies.

(5) *Federalized welfare system.* State and local governments in 1971 paid about half, or about $8 billion, of the total cost of welfare

programs. Some persons reasoned that by having the federal government assume all welfare costs, that much money would be released to state and local governments for other uses. This was the approach suggested by Senator Muskie in his March speech to the mayors when he said federalizing the welfare programs might be politically more acceptable than revenue sharing.

At first glance the idea of federalizing welfare as an alternative to tax sharing appeared to make good fiscal sense. Politically, however, it was on unfirm ground. One reason was that governors and mayors wanted badly to establish the principle of revenue sharing to get their foot into the door of the federal Treasury. Too, many cities would not directly benefit. Tax sharing would mean new, untied federal dollars going directly to the cities. On the other hand, many cities have no direct welfare burden, these costs being carried by state and county governments, and thus those cities would not receive a direct dollar benefit from a federalized welfare program. Finally, a federalized welfare program would disproportionately benefit a small number of states that pay high welfare payments—such as New York, California, and Massachusetts—with much less benefit to many other states. This alternative to tax sharing therefore had little political appeal among the organized interests lobbying for revenue sharing.

This was the overall view of alternative bills and approaches to tax sharing that confronted Congress when the time for the Mills hearings arrived.

CHAPTER VI

Congress Enacts a Law

In Congress, committee hearings on proposed legislation are an important, but often overrated, part of the legislative process. The hearing provides a forum for proponents and opponents to air their views, thus giving witnesses the psychological satisfaction that they and their constituents are being heard and their views are being considered. And, if the legislation is important enough, there may be television and newspaper reporters to convey these views to the public and provide publicity for hearing participants. Ideally, the hearings will also help to clarify some of the fundamental issues involved, such clarification perhaps benefiting not only committee members, but also the *interested* public. Congressional hearings on legislation are thus heavily laden with public relations and symbolic functions, for both committee members and witnesses, and should not be expected to bear a much heavier burden. Frequently, as was the case with revenue sharing, the most significant thing about legislative hearings is the fact that they are held, thus giving a bill a start through the legislative process. (Hearings on pending legislation are distinguished here from investigative hearings on matters such as Watergate, organized crime, or legislative oversight hearings, where additional functions may be served.)

In hearings on proposed legislation, the views of witnesses are generally well known in advance and the positions of the Committee members are often predetermined. This does not mean that the Committee members will not change their minds, but if they do it is generally the result of events occurring or pressures exerted outside of the formal hearing process. In short, the actual legislative hearings themselves seldom change any minds.

The House Ways and Means Committee hearings on general revenue sharing started on June 2. But before the major hearing began, a preliminary side scenario was played out in the Senate. Muskie, Chairman of the Intergovernmental Relations Subcommittee, got the jump on Mills by holding hearings on his bill and the Humphrey-Reuss proposal on June 1, a day ahead of Mills. The Muskie hearings had several apparent purposes: (1) to capitalize on revenue sharing publicity generated by the forthcoming House hearings; (2) to give advocates of tax sharing a friendly Congressional forum to offset the anticipated unfriendly House proceedings; (3) to signal to the mayors that Muskie still favored revenue sharing.

It was very clear, however, that the principal arena for the conflict was the House Ways and Means Committee. Spokesmen for the Nixon administration did not present testimony at the Muskie hearings, and many of the witnesses who did appear in the first days of the Senate proceedings were governors and mayors in Washington to present their views before the Mills committee.

The Mills hearings opened at 10 A.M. on June 2 with Treasury Secretary John B. Connally as the leadoff witness. The final witness, Mrs. Cassandra Gatlin, Director of the East Akron (Ohio) Neighborhood Center, gave her statement on June 28. By the time the hearings had ended, the committee had compiled more than 1,500 pages of testimony and supporting evidence.[1] Numerically, the number of witnesses was very heavily weighted on the side of tax sharing.

Secretary Connally's presentation was a broad-based support of the Nixon plan, buttressed with arguments against the two major alternatives—federalized welfare and tax credits. There were no surprises. Just about everything had already been said. Connally's case for tax sharing was based on the two major points that had become the standard approach: the financial crises pressing on state and local governments, and the need to shift decision-making authority away from the federal bureaucracy to state and local officials, with whom people have closer connections.

Importantly, in his statement Connally also stressed that revenue sharing was conceived as additional money:

> Contrary to many inaccurate reports, the $5 billion program of general revenue sharing will neither require a rise in tax rates nor a reduction in any existing Government programs.
>
> .   .   .   .
>
> As the money will be in addition to existing programs, each State, city and county will benefit directly: Each will receive revenue sharing money in addition to any benefits, services, or money it is now obtaining from the Federal Government.[2]

It thus was a firm commitment from the administration that general revenue sharing was not to be a substitute for other programs.

Connally also made the point that Nixon's total revenue sharing program would provide a better mix of federal assistance than the long-established categorical grant system. He noted that virtually all of the $30 billion in federal aid provided in fiscal year 1971 took the form of narrow, categorical grants. The Nixon program, including both general and special revenue sharing, would make a major realignment of aid forms. If Nixon's total revenue sharing package were adopted by Congress, Connally told the Committee, it would mean about 10 percent of aid taking the form of general revenue sharing with maximum flexibility on its use, 26 percent going out as special revenue sharing with flexibility within broad categories, and only 64 percent in categorical assistance with limited or no flexibility.

> Continued exclusive use of categorical assistance is neither an effective nor an equitable approach to the problems we face. The selective, subjective, fragmented, and over controlled nature of this approach is clearly not responsive to the need for more generalized and flexible assistance.[3]

This advocacy of a fiscal mix as opposed to continued reliance on the categorical approach pointed up a fundamental conflict to be observed in the hearings. There was prevailing agreement among most witnesses that state and local governments needed more financial aid. But there was a basic disagreement on how this assistance should be provided.

Andrew J. Biemiller, spokesman for the AFL-CIO and second witness at the hearings, put the distinction clearly:

> So the issue is not whether the Federal Government should share its revenues with the States and localities. On that there is not disagreement. The issue before this committee and before the Nation is the method of distribution and sharing.
>
> .   .   .   .
>
> The present method of categorical grants-in-aid transfers Federal funds to a State or local government for specific purposes or "categories," geared to high priority needs determined by Federal legislation. Such programs are established by the Congress, through the normal process of legislation and appropriation, with the opportunity for congressional review of how the programs are working.
>
> .   .   .   .
>
> *There is no justification for adoption of a new Federal aid delivery system which is specifically designed to bypass the process of congressional legislation, appropriation and oversight* [emphasis added].[4]

It was a clear appeal to Congressional prejudice against any proposal tending to diminish the powers of Congress as a whole and Congressional committees in particular. Biemiller went on to say:

> America needs a long-range national effort to greatly expand and improve public investments in facilities and services. This is beyond

question. Planned public programs will be required throughout the remainder of this century to revitalize the Nation's urban areas as centers of American civilization, and to improve the quality of life of the American people.[5]

Thus the issue between the Nixon administration and many Congressional opponents of revenue sharing, who were in accord with Biemiller on this point, was clearly drawn. Should the federal government relinquish to state and local officials its authority to establish priorities for programs funded with federal revenues? If some agreement existed between the two sides on fiscal needs, there was none on this political issue. Congressional liberals shared with some conservatives the basic, but not monolithic, belief, that the federal government must continue to establish national program priorities, fund them, and retain control over the expenditures. The federal government must not permit both the money and the policy-making authority to descend to state and local officials, who were buffeted and pressured by a host of parochial political and economic interests.

This political issue, implicit in the tax sharing controversy since 1964, remained a barrier to agreement in 1971. It divided the Nixon administration from many Congressional liberals and some conservatives, but it was not the only basis of opposition to tax sharing expressed at the hearing. There was also a cost argument, coming primarily from the business community and fiscal conservatives.

When Walter Heller proposed a revenue sharing program in mid-1964, he linked the distribution to anticipated revenue surpluses in the federal treasury. While this initial connection with surpluses was soon dropped by Heller, the concept of tax sharing was never able to completely shake its identification with budget surpluses. Thus, in the eyes of some, revenue sharing could only be considered feasible if the budget was at least balanced. Instead of balanced budgets, however, there was a series of deficits that grew larger during the first few years of the Nixon administration. By

1972, the annual budget deficit had passed $20 billion. In this budgetary setting, revenue sharing was certain to run up against the issue of financing. This was the point made by several witnesses during the House hearings and subsequently on the House floor when the legislation was brought up for a vote.

William Winter, spokesman for the U.S. Chamber of Commerce, said his organization opposed revenue sharing on several grounds, a major one being that it could only be financed through tax increases:

> It must be realized that general revenue sharing is nothing more than a new form of Government spending, and to the extent that this new form of spending does not replace other spending, there will be a need for increased taxes. I wonder how many Americans would favor general revenue sharing if it were now coupled with the tax rate increases that will ultimately be required to pay for it.[6]

Winter also touched on the issue of using revenue sharing as a substitute for existing grants instead of a supplement for them. Many Republican advocates of revenue sharing in the 1965-68 period supported substitution, and President Nixon apparently had not abandoned it despite public positions to the contrary. Though dormant, it was thus not a dead argument, and a number of tax sharing opponents shared Winter's view that

> If general revenue sharing were to be financed by substituting it for other Federal spending programs, such as categorical grants-in-aid, there might be some justification for suggesting that, to the extent of that substitution, there would be no need for future tax increases to pay for the program. But this is not the case. General revenue sharing is to be financed with new money, and is to start in a year when the Federal Government, by all reasonable estimates, will spend well in excess of its income.[7]

Marvin L. McLain, Legislative Director of the American Farm Bureau Federation, spoke in a similar tone in opposing the Nixon plan, saying,

> In the first place we must ask: "What revenue is to be shared?"
>
> At a time when the Federal Government is talking of sharing Federal

revenues with State and local government, it is noteworthy that the Federal Government does not have enough tax generated revenues to support itself.[8]

The Farm Bureau said it supported the tax credit approach to aiding state and local governments.

It was apparent in the hearings that tax sharing was being opposed by an unusual coalition of groups that traditionally were opposed to each other on many, if not most, issues. Labor, with its traditional liberal views on government policy and spending, found itself opposing a new spending program along with such traditionally conservative organizations as the U.S. Chamber of Commerce and the American Farm Bureau Federation. While there was unity in their opposition, they were opposing it for very different reasons, reasons that were consistent with their customary viewpoints. Labor was opposed to federal divestment of policy-making authority, while the Chamber and the Farm Bureau feared new deficits and consequent tax increases. This illustrates a fundamental principle of public policy making—that different issues bring together different coalitions of support and opposition. In the making of public policy there are few, if any, permanent coalitions.

A further aspect worth noting in the hearings was the stand taken by public employee organizations. A major concern of some opponents of revenue sharing had been that much of the shared money would be drained off for pay increases for powerful public employee groups and that little money would find its way down to the politically and economically disadvantaged in the form of facilities or services. The hearings indicated that some major public worker groups were eyeing this money as a source for just such pay increases.

In a statement presented for W. H. McClennan, President of the International Association of Fire Fighters, it was clear that this major labor group wanted federal money for pay raises and that revenue sharing would serve this purpose.

> . . .locals of the firefighters union are finding it disturbingly difficult to get the most minimal kind of pay adjustment—enough money to keep pace with the inflationary rise in prices.
>
> .　　.　　.　　.　　.　　.　　.　　.　　.　　.
>
> We appeal to this committee to take steps to provide Federal funds for the cities. Specifically, we ask that funds be made available for the protection services, both fire and police. . . .
>
> We have given general support to the concept of revenue sharing, but we are less concerned with the technicality of the approach than with the substance of the assistance.[9]

The firefighters were followed by Royce L. Givens, Executive Director of the International Conference of Police Associations, who also linked the financial assistance of revenue sharing with the pay needs of the nation's policemen.[10]

It is perhaps suggestive of how the revenue sharing issue had evolved that the sole case for the poor was made, most poignantly, by the last witness to appear, Mrs. Gatlin from the East Akron, Ohio, poverty office:

> . . . I am saying to this committee and to everybody in Washington: How could you even think about passing a revenue sharing bill that is going to say, "You take the money, to State or city or anywhere else, and do what you want with it."
>
> What will happen to poor people? In the city where I live they may as well jump into the river right now, because that is what will happen.
>
> .　　.　　.　　.　　.　　.　　.　　.　　.　　.
>
> I know that this plan was designed primarily to destroy Federal programs. I have heard all kinds of people with big degrees talk about it. But let me tell you something: Who did anything for the poor before the Federal Government came in? Who helped us? We had States and cities all along. Look at where the money went.
>
> What did the poor people get? Nothing. You went year after year, day after day, begging, and you received nothing.[11]

THE MILLS BILL:
POLITICS OF BILL WRITING

One of the most critical stages in a bill's legislative progress comes after the hearings end, when the committee (or sub-committee) goes into closed-door executive sessions. In some cases the hearings may be the last ever heard of a bill; the public relations function has been served, but there is little enthusiasm for the bill either in the hearing committee or in the House or Senate as a whole. In such cases the committee may spare everyone further dis-comfort by quietly burying the bill. If, however, the bill must be given serious consideration, two major concurrent and interrelated events take place in the committee. First, a final version of the bill must be written, along with a committee report. The final com-mittee bill may be the same as the bill originally introduced, or ma-jor changes may be needed. In either event, a coalition-building process begins to unfold simultaneously. Especially if major changes are necessary, amendments are made to build support for the final product, support in the form of a committee (or sub-committee) majority sufficient to move the legislation to the next stage in the legislative process. It is during this coalition-building that lobbying groups are especially active in seeking to influence committee members. The revenue sharing bill was typical of this committee amendment and coalition-building process.

The major target for lobbyists was Chairman Mills. On January 25, 1971, Mills had agreed to hold hearings for the purpose of killing revenue sharing. On May 11, he had predicted the plan would not be approved by his committee or Congress.[12] On June 2, following Secretary Connally's opening statement at the hearings, Mills retorted, "I want to congratulate you on making a very fine statement in behalf of a very weak cause."[13] On April 18, 1972, the Ways and Means Committee approved a $30 billion revenue sharing bill with Chairman Mills voting with the 18-7 majority.

Prospects for some kind of legislation brightened suddenly about a week after the hearings started, when Mills held a closed meeting with a group of Democratic officeholders from around the nation.[14] Attending the meeting were two governors, three mayors, two Senators, and Democratic National Committee Chairman

Lawrence O'Brien. During the session, Mills told the group of a possible alternative to the Nixon administration proposal. The alternative plan included some very substantial differences: (1) The money would be for local governments only; the states would receive nothing. (2) The program would provide $3.5 billion the first year. (3) It would be limited to three to five years. (4) The allotments would be on the basis of need, which had not been a direct factor in the Nixon plan. (5) The money could be used only for broad, specified purposes, with nothing permitted for capital expenditures.

From this point on revenue sharing shifted from the politics of the impossible to the politics of the possible, as Mills' position began to change from one of opposition to one of advocacy. At the same time, the substance of the legislation itself changed to meet the objections that Mills and others had about the Nixon plan. Lobbyists for revenue sharing now found themselves working in a more receptive environment than they had in the past.

Why this shifting of attitudes? First, the pressure from the mayors and governors was becoming more intense, as they began to feel that they were on the threshold of success and what was now required was pressing their views home with Mills and other Ways and Means Committee members. Second, and perhaps more important, Mills had begun to contemplate the possibility of becoming a Democratic candidate for President. The supporting base for such a candidacy could be the local Democratic leaders, especially elected officials, who formed the building blocks of local and state political parties. Mills was in a key position to develop some political credit with them by becoming a champion of their favorite cause. Certainly, it could be assumed, continued opposition to revenue sharing was untenable for any serious Presidential candidate. The presence of O'Brien at the meeting reflected the fact that revenue sharing was no longer being studied in isolation from national political currents and Presidential politics. Mills gave further credence to his reported interest in the nomination by more extensive traveling around the country and by making it a point to meet with local officials and local business leaders during his visits. (His formal candidacy was announced in March 1972.) Richard Thompson, the Washington lobbyist for the mayors, acquired Mills' travel schedule and made it a point for him to be greeted by mayors at every opportunity. It was intended as a mutually rewarding arrangement both for Mills and the nation's mayors. The period June through November 1971 was most critical to the prospects for revenue sharing, for it was during this six months, while Mills was out exploring his own political prospects, that he became committed to having some kind of legislation enacted. His commitment became firm on November 30 when he introduced his own version of tax sharing, H.R. 11950, the "Intergovernmental Fiscal Coordination Act of 1971."

The June-November period was marked by intensive lobbying by the mayors, county leaders, and governors. The latter had been greatly disturbed at the June meeting by Mills' alternative program excluding the states. In his testimony before the Ways and Means Committee on June 16, Rockefeller said that direct federal aid to cities, bypassing the states, would bring about "ultimately an end to the federal system of government as we know it."[15] Bypassing the states was likely also to break up the coalition that had been painfully built in support of revenue sharing.

Following the hearings, the Ways and Means Committee began a series of closed-door meetings to work out details of the Mills program. The committee was badly split, both ideologically and on specifics. Some, like ranking Republican John Byrnes, were opposed to the concept of revenue sharing. Others, while favorably disposed toward the idea, were concerned about how the money would be distributed. From the outset of the closed meetings one fact was clear to all participants—the Nixon plan had no chance. Lobbyists thus turned their attention to the drafting of a new plan and were very active in discussions with Mills and other committee members and staff who had responsibility for working out the details of the bill. A key person was Laurence Woodworth, staff director of the Joint Committee on Internal Revenue Taxation. This committe's staff is made up of a highly competent group of lawyers and economists whose job is to give technical assistance on tax legislation to both the Ways and Means Committee and the Senate Finance Committee.[16] A narrow view of the committee staff's function, however, masks its real importance. Much of its influence lies in the fact that it serves as a link between the two tax writing committees of Congress. Thus, Woodworth, as the chief of the Joint Committee staff, was also a go-between for the two powerful committee chairmen, Mills and Senator Russell Long of Louisiana. Woodworth was thus frequently involved in legislative matters going beyond the narrow confines of the work of the Joint Committee. Such was the case with the revenue sharing legislation, and Woodworth and the specialists on his staff were heavily courted by and worked closely with lobbyists representing the mayors and the governors, particularly Thompson for the mayors, James Martin for the National Governors Conference, and James Cannon, a Special Assistant to New York Governor Nelson Rockefeller. A major concern for everyone was Mills' statement that the money should go only to local governments.

In his January speech to the House, Mills had presented the view that the root of the fiscal difficulty for state and local governments was the urbanization process. The impact of urbanization fell primarily on local government, which had to provide such services as police and fire protection, refuse disposal, sewage systems, and street and mass transit systems. Sources of revenue for local governments were seriously limited, tied as they were primarily to the not easily expanded property tax, while their expenditures were about two-thirds of the state and local total. The case for the states was less persuasive, and it was felt by Mills and some other Committee members that Congressional efforts should be directed toward encouraging the states to solve their own revenue problems by better utilization of their larger tax bases, particularly the income tax. The effect of this line of reasoning was that when the Ways and Means Committee began executive meetings and when the staff began the work of rewriting the Nixon bill, they were immediately confronted with the revived problem of the cities *v.* the states. A local-government-only bill was never seriously considered, but Mills' statements did create some tensions within the pro-revenue sharing coalition. Publicly, Mills himself was quite optimistic about the prospects for his version, and in early July he predicted that a bill would be approved by the Committee in three weeks.[17] Elsewhere, it was already considered certain that the plan must include the states. On July 23, with the three week period coming to an end, the Committee was nowhere near agreement, and Mills once again expressed opposition to including the states in the plan.[18]

Meanwhile, the Administration, sensing that some kind of legislation might emerge from the Democratic-controlled Congress, began to revise its own bill to meet the demands of the large cities.[19] The original Nixon proposal tended to favor wealthy suburbs with high taxes, since the Administration formula based the distribution within a state on the relative amounts of general revenues raised. The results were some glaring inequities: for example, Beverly Hills, California, one of the nation's richest suburbs, would receive $24.30 per capita under the Nixon formula while the city of Los Angeles would receive only $12.33. To meet such problems and to make its plan more acceptable to the cities, the Treasury Department began trying out new formula combinations introducing some measure of need. The result was to redress some of the imbalances between the more needy central cities and the wealthier suburbs. On some points Mills, urban members of the Ways and Means Committee, and the Administration were coming closer together in their views about what kind of plan was acceptable. But, despite the narrowing of the gap between the Congress and the Administration, the major question of state participation remained.

It was apparent that unless the states were included in the program the prospects for revenue sharing legislation were not bright. There was intensive pressure from Rockefeller and other governors and from some members of the committee. It was also clear to the mayors and their lobbyists that the states had to be included in any legislation. Agreement was reached in H.R. 11950, introduced by Mills, which limited the program to five years and established a fixed sum of money, $5.3 billion, to be distributed annually.* Of this amount, $3.5 billion (two-thirds) was to go to local governments and $1.8 billion to the states. One growth factor was built in. The state funds would increase by $300 million a year, the additional funds to go to states increasing their tax collections. Without the growth funds a state could have been rewarded for instituting or increasing its income tax only at the expense of another state. In the final year of the five-year period of the program, therefore, the funds allocated for the states would have increased to about $3 billion, for a total state and local distribution of approximately $6.5 billion.

H.R. 11950 included another basic change from the Administration plan. The bill designated certain high priority expenditure categories. This change was a necessary condition of gaining the support of Mills and other persons who had fundamental objections to the "blank check" nature of the Heller-Pechman approach adopted by Nixon. To assure that local governments would not simply substitute revenue sharing money for local funds within the high priority categories, H.R. 11950 included the further provision that local officials had to maintain their own expenditure levels in these areas. The eligible expenditure categories were: maintenance and operating expenses for public safety (including law enforcement, fire protection, and building code enforcement), environmental protection (including

---

*H.R. 11950 was cosponsored by nine Democratic members of the Ways and Means Committee: Ullman, Burke, Rostenkowski, Vanik, Fulton of Tennessee, Corman, Green, Carey, and Karth.

sewage disposal, sanitation, and pollution abatement), public transportation (including transit systems and streets), youth recreation programs, health, financial administration; capital expenditures for sewage collection and treatment, refuse disposal systems, public transportation (including transit systems and street construction), the acquisition of open space for parks and public facilities, urban renewal programs. The major programs omitted were education and welfare, which, it was felt, were receiving sufficient federal assistance through other legislation. It should be noted that capital expenditures were included despite Mills' original opposition. Such expenditures are very popular because they offer physical evidence of how government is spending its money. Also, with a five year limit on the program, local officials did not want to have all of the money tied to maintenance and operating budgets and then to find this source of money, which tends to become locked into incremental budget decisions, disappearing at the end of the fifth year.

With these basic changes the substance of the legislation was now compatible with Mills' broadened political horizons. But, in the process of accommodating politics and principles, what had emerged was not revenue sharing but a multipurpose grant program. Conceptually, revenue sharing had been underpinned by essential elements of payments out of the federal income taxes and growing along with them, an indefinite commitment to permit long-range planning and, finally, a no strings approach. The bill introduced by Mills on November 30 was counter to these features, but what emerged and evolved continued to be called revenue sharing.

The states had succeeded in getting back into the program, and additional concessions were made to them to counterbalance the weighting of benefits to local officials. Among the compromises made toward the states was that the money going to the governors did not have to be used in the high priority categories; that is, the $1.8 billion (which was to increase in subsequent years) to the states was given with no strings. In addition, if a state was spending more on a program than the local governments, it could further define the categories of local spending on that program. The states were also permitted, under certain conditions, to enact legislation providing for different allocations of the local money within the states. Lobbyists for the mayors balked at certain of those concessions giving the states directive authority over local officials, but the compromise in H.R. 11950 was reached when it became apparent that without some trade offs there would be no legislation.

Another problem in producing the legislative package was the distribution formula among the state and local governments. The Mills bill linked a state's entitlement entirely to the amount of money collected from state income taxes, thus providing a strong incentive for states to adopt or increase income taxes. This provision, part of the price paid by the states for reinstatement, was not well received by some states, particularly those with no income tax. The impact of Presidential politics was felt on this part of the formula. In mid-February Mills went to New Hampshire where a Mills-for-President write-in campaign was being conducted in the weeks before the March 7 primary election. New Hampshire, with no income tax, was particularly sensitive to the income tax incentive provision, and Mills was under considerable pressure on this point during his visit there. In an apparent concession to political necessities, Mills told New Hampshire legislators that the incentive provision "must be changed and I shall urge that it be changed so states that act frugally, like you do here in New Hampshire, will not be penalized."[20] (In the revised revenue sharing bill, H.R. 14370, approved by the Ways and Means Committee in April 1972, the formula for the state allotments was altered, combining the income tax with a state's general tax collections as the measure of a state's tax effort. The Nixon plan had proposed distribution of the money among states according to a formula based largely on population, with a bonus going to states that taxed their citizens most heavily. Thus the House version was more clearly aimed at creating incentives for the states to make a greater effort to solve their own fiscal problems.)

At the local level, the Administration formula was based on the ratio between what a particular unit of local government raised in revenues from its own sources and the total of all locally collected revenues in the state. There was no equalization or "need" factor in the original Nixon proposal. The Mills bill revised this to base half of the local distribution on poverty—that is, on the number of low income families in the locality. This tended to weight the local distribution toward the rural south with its concentrations of poor families and toward the large cities of the country. The bill did not provide aid to local governments serving less than 2,500 people. With the poverty factor, which biased the formula in favor of the south and the large cities, and the cutoff of the smaller communities, the most pressure for further change in the local allocation provisions came from Committee members from northern states, especially those representing metropolitan suburbs and scattered rural constituencies. Changes in the Mills formula were supported by the urban lobby.

Introduction of the Mills bill carried revenue sharing a long way toward further House action, but there was continued disagreement in the Committee over the distribution of money among the states, which caused continued delays in final Committee action on the legislation. There was also the problem that within the Committee there remained some strong opposition to any bill at all. This opposition included Byrnes; on the Democratic side it was led by Congressman Sam Gibbons of Florida (whose state did not have an income tax), who disliked both the idea of revenue sharing and the distribution formulas that were being proposed. On March 6, (more than three months after introducing his bill and one day before the New Hampshire primary), in a speech to the National League of Cities-U.S. Conference of Mayors, Mills openly urged the mayors to step up their lobbying with Congressmen.

> I need some help, and I need it in the Ways and Means Committee.
> Don't leave the city of Washington until you make a personal appeal
> to those members of Congress you can talk to. Talk especially to Ways
> and Means Committee members.[21]

It was an unusual plea and showed Mills' complete alignment
with the mayors behind revenue sharing, a reversal of his position
of less than a year earlier. His remarks also showed that, despite his
influence within the Committee, he was continuing to encounter
significant resistance. His change of position clearly indicates that
the study of how bills become laws is not the study of any tidy,
linear process.

Over the next five weeks work continued on a new bill (H.R.
14370), and some further changes were made in the legislation.
Among the major changes was the elimination of the income tax
incentive as the sole criterion for a state's allocation. Significant
changes were also made in the local distribution formula to aid
large urban areas, which were well represented on the Committee.
The two-thirds to be allocated among the states for direct federal
distribution to local governments within the states would be
decided by a formula based one-third on population, one-third on
"urbanized" population, and one-third on population weighted
by inverse relative per capita income.* The specific distributions
within a state to county, municipal, and township governments
would be based on the same type of complex formula. It was
provided, however, that after a year and a half a state legislature
could enact a law altering, within limits, the weight of these three
factors in distribution of the money within the state. Adding the
urbanized population factor, which was suggested by the Joint
Committee staff as a means of counterbalancing the rural bias of
H.R. 11950, was expected to benefit the metropolitan suburbs,
since these communities were the areas of greatest population

---

*"Urbanized" population was defined as cities of 50,000 or over and the
metropolitan areas surrounding them. This is distinguished from an "urban"
area, which is defined by the Census Bureau as a community with 2,500 or more
persons.

growth. While designing the formula to favor the more populated communities (and thus meeting the demands of a majority of the Committee), it was also agreed to extend the benefits to all units of local government without regard to a population limit. The only limit was that no payment of less than $200 would be made, leaving out only those communities with 15 or 20 residents. The combination of these agreements made the proposal satisfactory to suburban and rural representatives and to the lobbying organizations.

There were other important features in the new bill:

(1) The effect of the priority expenditure categories was largely negated when the committee eliminated the requirement that local governments maintain previous levels of expenditure in the specified areas. Without this local maintenance of effort provision, local officials were now free to substitute revenue sharing money for their own funds within the specified categories. For example, with a maintenance of effort requirement, a city spending an average of $200,000 a year for police salaries before revenue sharing would have to maintain this level, and revenue sharing money could only be *added* to this for salary increases. Without the maintenance of effort, it would be possible to shift the $200,000 over to a nonpermissible area such as education and pay all of the police salaries from revenue sharing money. In short, with such substitution a possibility, the expenditure categories had very little meaning.

(2) There was a maintenance-of-effort provision at the state level. To get their money, the states must continue to distribute as much from other sources to local governments as they did in fiscal year 1971. This is, states were not permitted to cut their own aid to local governments now that local officials were receiving the new federal money.

(3) No Congressional action on appropriations would be required for the five-year lifetime of the bill. The legislation, once passed, would constitute a permanent appropriation for each of

the five years the program would be in effect. Once the idea of linking shared revenues automatically with the income tax base was dropped, this was an extremely important provision, for elimination of this linkage would have placed the new version of revenue sharing at the mercies of the annual budget and appropriation process with no certainty that the amount authorized would be requested by the President or provided by Congress. But, by building in the permanent appropriation safeguard, the Ways and Means Committee was now open to the charge of invading the jurisdiction of the Appropriations Committee. The Ways and Means Committee does have the authority to make permanent appropriations in some tax-related areas such as Social Security, but with tax sharing disconnected from tax legislation the basis for the committee's authority to make the permanent appropriation was more questionable. The new version of revenue sharing was seen as a multipurpose grant program, and this became the source of some antagonism when the bill was brought to the floor for a vote. This point in the eyes of some House members, particularly members of the Appropriations Committee, was that the Ways and Means Committee was engaged in a legislative power grab.

REVENUE SHARING PASSES THE HOUSE

On April 17, the Ways and Means Committee met and gave its final approval to the revised plan, H.R. 14370, the "State and Local Fiscal Assistance Act of 1972."[22] The Committee vote was 18 to 7. The vote was across party lines with Republicans and Democrats voting on both sides. The opposition based its arguments on a number of points, including the constitutionality of the bill and the fact that there were no revenues to share. The dissenting views included many of the arguments that had blocked revenue sharing from serious consideration between the years 1964 and 1971, but the issue environment had changed greatly between January 1971 and April 1972. It was an election year, the pressures for some kind of legislation had grown considerably, and principles yielded to the money and the politics.

It was two months from the time the Committee approved the bill that it came to the floor for consideration. During that two month period there was intensive lobbying for votes by the Administration, Congressional leaders, individual Representatives, and the state, county, and city organizations. The first lobbying effort was with the fifteen-member Rules Committee. Chairman William Colmer of Mississippi, who was planning to retire from Congress, was strongly opposed to revenue sharing and succeeded in delaying Rules Committee action for several weeks. But there was also difficulty with other members of the Committee. The point at issue was the "closed rule."

The mayors and governors, having worked strenuously to get an acceptable bill in the Ways and Means Committee, did not want to jeopardize their efforts by having the bill amended on the floor. They wanted to have the tax sharing legislation considered under a closed rule, thereby permitting no amendments to be made in the bill during floor consideration. The closed rule was also the customary way that legislation from the Ways and Means Committee was presented to the full house. Within the Rules Committee there was opposition to revenue sharing itself, so those votes for a closed rule were lost. But there was also some opposition from liberal Democrats on the committee who were philosophically opposed to the no-amendment procedure because it had been used too frequently in the past by conservative committee chairmen and the Rules Committee to block liberal amendments to legislation. Banning the closed rule procedure was part of a larger liberal package to reform the House, and they were reluctant to support it for revenue sharing. As a result of these differing pressures, the mayors and governors found themselves with a 7-7 split, with the key vote held by Representative Spark M. Matsunaga, a liberal Democrat from Hawaii who opposed the closed rule procedure. To put pressure on Matsunaga, Charles A. Byrley, Washington Office Director of the Council of State Governments, called Governor John A. Burns of Hawaii asking the governor to call Matsunaga for a favorable vote. Byrley found Burns himself cool toward revenue sharing, because the formula was not very favorable to the state government in Hawaii. Nevertheless, Burns agreed to call Matsunaga in behalf of the Council. He did so, and the final Rules Committee vote on May 23 was 8 to 7 with Matsunaga voting for the close rule.

After this success in the Rules Committee, the final coalition building process got under way for the floor vote. Once again, the closed rule was the key issue. In the procedures of the House it is necessary to approve the rule establishing the terms of debate and amendment before the substance of legislation can be considered. Therefore, the first opportunity that opponents of a bill have to defeat it on the floor is the vote on the rule itself. The rule vote frequently serves as a test vote on the legislation. Opponents of the revenue sharing legislation hoped that by defeating the closed rule on the floor enough amendments could be made in the legislation to splinter the support for revenue sharing and thereby break up the coalition that had been built for the program. Chairman George Mahon of the Appropriations Committee wanted to make revenue sharing subject to the regular appropriations process. Others hoped to use the revenue sharing legislation as a vehicle for tax reform, while still others wanted the opportunity to amend the distribution formulas. It was imperative, therefore, for proponents of revenue sharing to preserve the closed rule and prevent amendment strategies.

Once again the mayors and governors were at the front of the lobbying effort to round up floor votes in support of the closed rule. They concentrated on House Democrats, while Administration lobbyists worked on Republican members. Within the House, Mills and John M. Martin, Jr., Chief Counsel of the Ways and Means Committee, talked with Democratic members, as did Majority Leader Hale Boggs and his assistant. Minority Leader

Gerald Ford and Minority Whip Les Arends lined up Republican lawmakers. Some unexpected opposition lobbying appeared in the final weeks. On June 2 the U.S. Chamber of Commerce sent a memorandum to its members and friends urging them to press their Representatives to vote against the bill or have it returned to Committee for major changes. On June 9 the AFL-CIO sent a letter to House members saying it opposed the closed rule on revenue sharing, thus hoping to break off liberal Democratic support for the bill. While the AFL-CIO was opposing the closed rule, one of its major affiliates, the American Federation of State, County, and Municipal Employees, was lobbying in behalf of tax sharing. At one point the House leadership postponed action on the bill, believing it did not have the votes to win. Governor Rockefeller and representatives of other governors and mayors, having made their own vote count, met personally with Mills and House Speaker Carl Albert on June 13 and convinced them that there were enough votes to pass the bill. The margin was estimated at forty votes. H.R. 14370 was brought to the House floor on June 21 under a closed rule. The rule was adopted by a vote of 223 to 185, a thirty-eight-vote margin and just two under the vote estimate of the mayors and governors.

The bill then had to be accepted as reported by the Ways and Means Committee or there would be no legislation. With the closed rule preventing amendments upheld, it became certain that the bill would pass the House. From that point on opposition dwindled (only 10 of the 55 members of the Appropriations Committee voted for the rule; 30 voted "yes" on final passage). The following day a motion to send the bill back to committee for changes (and thereby kill it) was defeated 241 to 157. On the final vote, revenue sharing passed the House 275 to 122. It was passed with bipartisan support, 153 Democrats and 122 Republicans voting for the bill, and 80 Democrats and 42 Republicans against it.

The voting showed the distance tax sharing legislation had

moved over the years. As brought out in earlier chapters, tax sharing in the past had received its strongest support from the more conservative members of the House and tended to be opposed most strongly by liberal lawmakers who saw it as a device for ending many grant-in-aid programs and who distrusted putting "no strings" money in the hands of state and local officials. In 1967, the "substitute" approach had become the position of the Republican leadership in the House. The Nixon bills of August 1969 and January 1971 had divided the issue along party lines, with few Democrats sponsoring the Administration proposal though some had their own versions.

But as the prospects for tax sharing became brighter after June 1971, lawmakers had to distinguish between their general attitudes toward such legislation, the specifics of the legislation itself, and the political environment of an election year in which revenue sharing was being considered. For fiscal conservatives, many of whom supported revenue sharing in earlier years, a commanding fact was that tax sharing was seen in 1971 as a new spending program, coming at a time when budget deficits were exceeding $20 billion a year. This group saw revenue sharing as requiring new taxes. For many liberals, the pressure for the new money from some of their strongest political allies, the big city mayors, was too great to resist. The result was that the relatively homogeneous clusters of support and opposition that had formed when passage was *not* a likely possibility rearranged themselves as the prospects for enactment improved.

In 1972, voting support in the House for revenue sharing came from both liberals and conservatives, defined by their ratings from the Americans for Constitutional Action (conservative) and the Americans for Democratic Action (liberal).[23] (The ACA opposed revenue sharing for fiscal reasons; ADA spokesman Paul Parks supported the program during the Senate hearings).

The crucial vote was on the closed rule, adopted 223 to 185. The no-amendment rule was supported by two-thirds of the

Republicans (113-57), but only 46 percent of the Democrats (110-128). Two-thirds of the southern Democrats, the conservative wing of the party, voted against it (21-59). The northern Democratic vote was 89 to 69 for the closed rule. Northern Democrats, who tend to be the most liberal bloc in the House, apparently divided over the issue of supporting a procedural motion which ran counter to their reform position. To some extent, however, the position taken by individual northern liberals was the result of pressures within the state delegation, as indicated by the New York votes. Rockefeller and the New York House delegation (about 2 to 1 liberal) had long favored and worked for revenue sharing legislation, and the cohesion of the delegation was shown by the vote on the closed rule. Of the 38 New York House members voting on the closed rule, only two (Otis G. Pike and Shirley Chisholm, both liberal Democrats), voted against it. Only Pike subsequently voted against final passage.

An analysis of the closed rule vote on the conservative-liberal scale shows that the no-amendment procedure was adopted through the combined support of liberals (88) and conservatives (96), plus votes from House members who did not receive 50

TABLE IV

Conservative-Liberal Voting, Revenue Sharing Act,
House of Representatives, June 1972

	Closed Rule		Passage		No. in
	Yea	Nay	Yea	Nay	House*
ACA over 50%	96	115	114	92	224
ACA over 80%	36	73	37	64	112
ADA over 50%	88	51	117	20	148
ADA over 80%	39	27	55	12	70

Source: Data calculated from Americans for Constitutional Action, *ACA Index: An Analysis of the Voting Record of Each Member in the Congress of the United States, 1st Sess., 92nd Congress,* 1971, Washington, D.C.; Americans for Democratic Action, *ADA World,* Nov.-Dec. 1972, Washington, D.C.

*Numbers on individual votes may not equal the total number of the various categories in the House because some members did not have recorded votes.

percent ratings from either the ACA or ADA. This latter group provided 39 of the 223 votes for the closed rule. A closer study of the liberal-conservative vote showed that the more conservative the voting record of the member, the more he was likely to vote against the closed rule—a vote against the bill as written by the Committee. Members receiving an ACA conservative rating of 80 percent or more voted 2 to 1 against the closed rule; those with ratings from 50 to 79 percent voted 60 to 42 for the closed rule, in support of the Committee proposal. The most liberal vote was nearly the reverse of the most conservative vote, with almost 60 percent of those with liberal ADA ratings of 80 percent or more voting in favor of a closed rule.

On final passage, revenue sharing again drew the combined support of liberals and conservatives, with 114 conservatives and 117 liberals providing the winning majority. However, this represents a far greater proportion (79 percent) of the total liberal vote in the House than of the conservative vote (51 percent). The shift between the closed rule vote and final passage further illustrates the ideological blend found among supporters of the legislation. On final passage, revenue sharing had 52 more supporters than it had on the closed rule vote. Of these 52, 18 came from the conservatives and 29 from the liberals. Proportionately, this also represented a greater shift among the liberals, but some of the liberal "nay's" on the first vote were motivated by their reform views on closed rule procedures and were not votes against revenue sharing itself. The essential point is that the revenue sharing bill written by the Ways and Means Committee had gained both wide ideological and bipartisan acceptability, a reflection of "the something for everybody" nature of the bill.

There was more ideological homogeneity among those voting against tax sharing. Of the 122 "nay" votes, a total of 92 (75 percent) came from persons with ACA conservative ratings above 50 percent. Of this 92, there were 64 with ACA ratings of 80 percent or more. Only 37 members with ACA ratings over 80 percent voted for revenue sharing. Thus the most conservative House members were nearly 2 to 1 opposed to tax sharing. Only 12 persons with liberal ADA ratings of 80 percent or more voted against tax sharing, while 55 with strong liberal credentials voted for passage. The clear balance of the most conservative members was thus against revenue sharing; the most liberal members voted nearly 5 to 1 in favor of the program.

What had occurred among the more conservative House members over the years was a significant split in their views about tax sharing. In previous years the conservative support for revenue sharing had been quite solid, but in 1972, 44 percent of the conservative House members voting on the issue voted against tax sharing. A substantial part of the support that the program had enjoyed in the past had shifted away. On the other hand, sharing picked up the support of many House liberals who had been wary of the program in the past. These members were the most responsive to the pressures from the mayors and governors who argued their case on the basis of fiscal need. With the repeated statements from the Administration that revenue sharing money would be in addition to other aid, the former opponents found their position weakened.

Put another way, the fiscal conservatives saw that revenue sharing, as redesigned, was not the radical overhaul of the aid system they had supported in 1967. Instead, it was perceived as the result of a political bargaining process, simply providing additional money in modified form. It was this same perception of the legislation that made H.R. 14370 less threatening in appearance to House liberals. In the end it was the House liberals, many who had long opposed tax sharing, who made sharing possible.

SENATE: POLITICS OF THE SHARING FORMULA

There are two basic kinds of federal grant program, the project grant and the formula grant. The former provides funds on the basis of an application for a particular project, and the application is considered on its merits. There are no guarantees that the money will be provided. Considerable administrative discretion is exercised by federal grant officials in allocating the money. Examples of project grants are urban renewal, public housing, and public works grants from the Economic Development Administration. Formula grants, on the other hand, are provided on the basis of certain objective criteria and, in most cases (welfare is one exception), a given amount of money is available annually for a given jurisdiction. For example, the 1956 highway program is a formula grant program; the amount of money allotted to each state is based partially on population and size of the state. The highway funds are earmarked for particular approved projects within a state, but the money for a given state is set aside and is not lost to the state unless it is not spent within a specified period of time.

Among the complaints about project grants is that, with the discretionary authority involved, the money is allocated on a first-come, first-served basis, thus frequently favoring the larger communities with the expertise to develop project ideas quickly and make the necessary applications. Formula grants, on the other hand, remove this problem, and states and communities do not have to compete with each other for a limited amount of money. It should not be presumed, however, that formula grants are neutral and unbiased. They are not intended to be. The formulas are based on criteria which are measures of such factors as population, income, area, and other quantified indicators. Thus, what criteria are used for the distribution of money is highly important, both fiscally and politically. For example, using population as a factor weights the distribution of money in favor of the most populated states and communities. Introducing the criterion of land area, as in the highway programs, gives a strong formula bias toward the large western states, many of which are sparsely populated. Use of a need factor such as income levels gives the formula a redistributive objective, favoring the poorer states and communities. In short, when Congress addresses itself to developing a formula grant program there is likely to be a political conflict over the criteria. Revenue sharing was based on a formula.

The distribution formulas adopted by the House included biases of several kinds. The formula for allotments to the states was based on a combination of income tax collections and the state's general tax effort. It was designed partially to encourage states without an income tax or with low rates to adopt such a tax or to raise the tax rate. This was immediately seen as biasing the formula against the ten states without an income tax—Connecticut, Florida, Nevada, New Hampshire, New Jersey, South Dakota, Tennessee, Texas, Washington, and Wyoming. Conversely, this favored such states as California and New York with large income tax collections.

The local distribution formula was based on combinations of population, urbanized population, and need as measured by relative income levels. These criteria partly reflected the analysis that the basic fiscal difficulty faced by state and local governments was the result of the urbanization process. Therefore, it was appropriate to weight the formula in favor of the most populated, urbanized states and communities. However, this bias of the House formula was more than a simple weighting of benefits toward the populated areas, based on a particular perception of the problem. The formula was also a clear reflection of institutional factors. The House approximates a one man, one vote institution, whereby the most populated states and communities enjoy a numerical advantage. The majority of the Ways and Means Committee members came from the most populous states. It was thus natural that the sharing formula would be weighted toward population. Moreover, by inserting the urbanized population criterion, the formula was further weighted toward the nation's metropolitan areas. This urbanization factor was particularly favorable toward the populous suburbs which frequently make up more than half of the population within a metropolitan area. The need factor of the formula redressed the bias toward the heavily urbanized states and shifted funds toward the poorer south. In addition, *within* states, the use of relative income favored the central cities over the suburbs. The House formula thus represented a political mix necessary to gain the support of city, suburban, and rural representatives. Even with these efforts to achieve political acceptability and to put the money where it was more needed, there was dissatisfaction with the thrust and complexity of the formula. During the floor debate James C. Corman, a liberal Democrat from California and a member of the Ways and Means Committee who opposed the bill, put the difficulties the Committee had in adopting the formula this way:

> We finally quit, not because we hit on a rational formula, but because we were exhausted. And finally we got one that almost none of us could understand at the moment. We were told the statistics were not available to run the [computer] print on it. So we adopted it, and it is here for you today.[24]

When H.R. 14370 went to the Senate Finance Committee, the conflict over the distribution formula was renewed, and now it faced different political and institutional pressures.* While the House membership is based on population distribution, the Senate reflects greater representation of states with smaller populations and fewer cities. As a result, when the Finance Committee began its revisions of the House bill, it started with some major changes in the distribution formula to accommodate different institutional demands. The general thrust of the Finance Committee efforts was to bias the bill more toward the south and rural areas. It was anticipated that in any subsequent House-Senate Conference Committee the Senate would then have some differences to compromise with the urban oriented House version. The professional staff of the Joint Committee was put in the position of having to undo some of its earlier work, since it had been their suggestion to include the "urbanized" population factor in the House bill to reduce the southern, rural bias.

---

*There was a companion Senate bill, S. 3651, to H.R. 14370, but the House version remained the principal bill throughout Congressional action.

One of the changes was to reduce the complexity of the House formulas. The House, in effect, had two separate formulas—one for the states and one for local governments. One result was that, while the aggregate figures provided one-third of the money to the states and two-thirds to local governments, within many states this division of shares was not achieved and many state governments received more than a third of the money.[25] (This was not necessarily bad since the division of functions between state and local governments varies widely—a criticism that was made of the uniform one-third, two-thirds split.) For example, the New York state government, under the House formula, received nearly 50 percent of the money. In some states, the state government's share fell well below one-third, as in Alabama, where less than 20 percent of the money went to the state.

Thus, motivated by political and institutional demands, the Senate committee scrapped much of the complex House approach and devised a single formula, applicable to both state and local governments, that would result in a uniform one-third, two-thirds distribution. The first House criterion to be eliminated was the income tax incentive, which had aroused the opposition of state governments. Secondly, the "urbanized" population factor was eliminated. The Senate formula became a three-factor one based on population, total tax effort, and need as measured by per capita income. Once the money was allocated to a state, then one-third of the total went to the state government and two-thirds was earmarked for county, municipal, and township distribution.

The overall effect was to hurt states, such as New York and California, with large income tax revenues. Neither was represented on the Finance Committee. By elimination of the income tax incentive, the ten states without such taxes were aided, as well as the less populous states which collect a smaller proportion of all income taxes. Elimination of the urbanized population factor further lowered the share of the most populous states and also reduced the allocations to the suburbs. On the other hand, elimination of the income tax incentive and the urbanized population criterion gave greater emphasis to the remaining factors—general tax effort, relative income, and population. By greater emphasis on relative income and tax effort, the suburbs lost further ground because their income levels tend to be higher than those of central cities and rural communities and because, in relation to their higher income levels, the suburbs tend to have a lower tax effort than central cities, where the tax burdens are generally higher. The net effect of the Senate formula was to make the distributions more favorable to the central cities and rural areas, particularly in the south. The Senate formula thus had a greater equalization effect than the House approach in that the former tended to direct more funds to the poorer areas. In all, 34 states got more in the Senate committee version than in the House bill; 16 got less. Of the 16 states represented on the Senate committee, 13 received more.

The Senate committee's work on tax sharing was complicated by an external issue that had emerged during the summer of 1972.[26] This involved social services grants under the Social Security Act. In 1962, Congress had enacted amendments to the Act providing 75 percent federal grants for a wide range of social services designed to reduce dependency on welfare. It was an open-ended, mandatory grant; that is, as in welfare assistance, there was no fixed annual amount the federal government would make available; it would simply provide matching funds for whatever services were provided at the state and local levels. For several years, state and local officials were not fully aware of the potential of the program in terms of the amount of money they could get from the federal government. This lack of awareness did not last, however, and the amount of money going out for social services started to grow appreciably. In fiscal year 1971, the grants totaled about $750 million; in fiscal year 1972 about $1.5 billion; and in 1973 they were expected to reach $4.7 billion. The cost had grown far beyond what the Administration and Congress had expected and were willing to continue. Therefore, it was felt that a limit had to be placed on the amount the federal government would make available annually. The revenue sharing bill in the Senate was selected as the vehicle for setting a limit on the social services grants. H.R. 14370 was chosen because it was a bill eagerly sought by state, county, and local officials and they would have to accept a limit on social services grants in exchange for the revenue sharing money. The governors and mayors, particularly from the urbanized states which had been getting most of the money, were very unhappy about this trade off, but they had little room for bargaining.

The social services grant issue thus became an integral part of the revenue sharing bargaining process. The Senate Finance Committee authorized, as part of the revenue sharing bill, a $1 billion annual social service grant program for a period of four years, for a total of $4 billion. This money would be distributed on the basis of urbanized population. By establishing the urbanized population criterion, the Committee sought to help out the urban states which had been hurt by its elimination in the revenue sharing part of the bill. Adding the supplemental social services money based on population to the other money reduced to four the number of states receiving less than in the House version. In addition to this $1 billion, $600 million was authorized for child care and family planning grants. The net effect of the Committee action was to set a $1.6 billion limit on the social services program, a figure well below the amounts being sought by state and local officials.

The Senate Finance Committee made some other changes in H.R. 14370.

(1) It eliminated the high priority expenditure categories of the House, thereby making it a "no strings" plan, as proposed by the Nixon administration.

(2) The $300 million annual growth money would be divided on a one-third, two-thirds basis like the rest of the money. The House bill proposed giving the entire $300 million a year to the states.

(3) The funds for revenue sharing and the social service grants

would be obtained by setting aside 7 percent of the individual federal income tax receipts in a trust fund, an approach in accord with the original concept of revenue sharing. This would have meant that the revenue sharing fund would expand along with national economic growth. It was apparent, however, that this was simply a legislative ploy to get around objections of the Appropriations Committee, because the Senate version, like the House bill, set an annual amount to be made available. If the 7 percent was in excess of the specified annual amounts, the excess was to be returned to the Treasury. An effort was made on the Senate floor to require annual appropriations after the first eighteen months of the program. This amendment, offered by Appropriations Committee Chairman John L. McClellan of Arkansas, was rejected by a vote of 49 to 34. In the subsequent House-Senate conference where the final differences were resolved, the Senate conferees readily agreed to the House version.

When the Finance Committee bill came to the Senate floor, a major point of disagreement was the distribution formula. Several efforts were made by Senators from urban states to amend the formula, but all such attempts were voted down. By substantial margins, the Senate rejected seven amendments favoring larger states, offered by Senators from Ohio, New York, and Connecticut. The Senate accepted a total of 11 minor amendments and rejected 19, including the attempts to change the distribution formula and to rewrite the financing provisions. On September 12, the Senate passed the amended version of H.R. 14370 by a vote of 64 to 20. The bill then went to conference.

FINAL AGREEMENT

It was evident that the Conference committee would come to a quick, friendly settlement on a compromise version of the bill in order to get final action before adjournment. The makeup of the conferees showed there would be little difficulty in getting their approval—only two of the twelve Representatives and Senators selected as conferees had voted against passage of the bill. Also, the elections were just six weeks away, and both Congress and the President wished to claim their share of political credit for having the legislation approved. While the predisposition for agreement was thus present, there was the difficult problem of resolving the differences in the distribution formulas. None of the five Senate conferees was from a large industrial state, and each of their states gained by use of the Senate formula. The House conferees, on the other hand, gave greater representation to larger states. Of the seven House members, only two (including Mills) represented states that would get more money from the Senate bill, while the states of the other five would lose funds. Thus, the diverse institutional orientations that had led to the original differences in the distribution formulas were carried over into the conference committee.

In a very unusual compromise, the conferees allowed each state the larger of the allocations its state and local governments would have received under the two versions.[27] This meant that the more populous, urbanized states would receive the higher allocations of the House formula while the smaller, less populous states would receive the amount carried in the Senate bill. This solution was first proposed by Cannon, Rockefeller's Special Assistant, who feared that any compromise that split the dollar differences between the House and Senate bills would result in New York's losing revenue sharing money. In allowing the maximum amounts to go to each state, the cost of the first year was increased to $5.8 billion, $500 million more than planned in either the House or Senate bills. To keep the first year total at $5.3 billion, each state's allocation was reduced proportionately for 1972.

While permitting the choice which would provide the maximum amounts of dollars to all governments within a state, the conferees did have to decide between the two sets of criteria to establish a formula whereby the money would be divided among the state and local governments. The conference committee decided in favor of the less complex Senate formula of population, tax effort, and relative income, which gave the state government one-third of the money within a state and the local governments two-thirds. The divisions among local governments within a state used variations of these same factors. The same apportionment was adopted for the annual increases, which the conferees reduced to $150 million a year instead of the $300 million that had been approved by both House and Senate. This cut reduced the overall cost of the bill over the five-year period.

Other major provisions of the bill adopted by the conferees were:

(1) The funds received by local governments were to be used only for the designated high priority spending categories. The final legislation, however, carried no local maintenance of effort provision, and thus local budget makers could shift their own revenues around in such a way as to make revenue sharing approximate a "no strings" approach. The categories (not applicable

TABLE V

Distribution of Aid Funds among the States under the House, Senate, and Enacted Formulas of H.R. 14370, for Calendar Year 1972 (in millions of dollars)

States	5 factor formula (House)	3 factor formula (Senate)	Enacted formula (higher of 3 or 5 factor formulas)	
			Before scaling to $5,300 mil.	After scaling to $5,300 mil.
United States, total	5,300.0	5,300.0	5,786.9	5,301.3
Alabama	73.1	98.9	98.9	90.6
Alaska	6.8	5.8	5.8	6.6
Arizona	46.6	54.8	54.8	50.2
Arkansas	38.4	60.0	60.0	54.5
California	611.7	517.4	611.7	560.3
Colorado	59.5	58.5	59.5	54.5
Connecticut	73.4	59.1	73.4	67.2
Delaware	17.5	13.4	17.5	16.1

TABLE V CONTINUED

District of Columbia	26.1	14.3	26.1	23.9
Florida	151.2	160.2	160.2	146.7
Georgia	103.4	119.7	119.7	109.6
Hawaii	25.9	21.9	25.9	23.7
Idaho	15.8	23.2	23.2	21.3
Illinois	299.2	248.6	299.2	274.0
Indiana	115.9	124.2	124.2	113.8
Iowa	66.9	82.4	82.4	75.5
Kansas	47.2	57.3	57.3	52.4
Kentucky	71.7	95.0	95.0	87.0
Louisiana	84.9	133.8	133.8	122.5
Maine	19.8	33.9	33.9	31.0
Maryland	116.9	92.2	116.9	107.1
Massachusetts	180.3	144.7	180.3	165.1
Michigan	245.0	220.8	245.0	224.4
Minnesota	116.2	113.1	116.2	106.4
Mississippi	45.7	96.6	96.6	88.4
Missouri	107.2	106.6	107.2	98.2
Montana	16.8	22.4	22.4	20.5
Nebraska	33.6	42.4	42.4	38.9
Nevada	12.6	12.1	12.6	11.5
New Hampshire	13.9	18.1	18.1	16.6
New Jersey	181.9	146.4	181.9	166.6
New Mexico	22.6	36.0	36.0	33.0
New York	643.0	501.2	643.0	589.0
North Carolina	113.4	148.5	148.5	136.0
North Dakota	12.3	24.2	24.2	22.2
Ohio	233.6	210.2	233.6	213.9
Oklahoma	52.8	64.3	64.3	58.9
Oregon	57.9	52.3	57.9	53.0
Pennsylvania	303.5	299.0	303.5	278.0
Rhode Island	26.4	25.0	26.4	24.2
South Carolina	55.4	78.7	78.7	72.1
South Dakota	13.3	26.3	26.3	24.1
Tennessee	79.4	107.9	107.9	98.9
Texas	249.5	270.7	270.7	247.9
Utah	28.8	33.4	33.4	30.6
Vermont	11.0	16.1	16.1	14.7
Virginia	116.1	110.4	116.1	106.3
Washington	77.5	85.1	85.1	78.0
West Virginia	36.5	56.7	56.7	52.0
Wisconsin	135.7	145.5	145.5	133.3
Wyoming	6.2	10.9	10.9	10.0

Source: U.S., Congress, Joint Committee on Internal Revenue Taxation, *General Explanation of the State and Local Fiscal Assistance Act,* Feb. 12, 1973, p.26.

to state governments) were maintenance and operating expenses for public safety, environmental protection, public transportation, health, recreation, libraries, social services for the poor or aged, and financial administration. Any capital expenditures were permitted.

(2) The Senate provisions for the supplemental social services grants were dropped. The compromise version established a flat $2.5 billion a year ceiling on social services grants for specified purposes. This was a more generous amount than had been provided in the Senate bill, but the distribution formula was less favorable to the highly urbanized states. The Senate had allocated the supplemental grants on the basis of urbanized population; the conference bill changed this to just "population."

(3) State and local governments could not use their revenue sharing money as matching funds for other federal grants. This was aimed at preventing the use of tax sharing money to escalate the demands for other federal grants.

(4) The bill carried a provision for federal collection of state income taxes if requested by state governments. In order to participate under this "piggy backing" provision, a state would have to make its income tax conform to the federal taxes, by making the state tax a percentage of the federal income tax or by applying the state income tax rates to the same base as the federal taxes.

On September 25 the conferees finished their work, establishing a five year program to share $30,236,400,000 in federal revenues with state and local governments. The effective date of the program was made retroactive to January 1, 1972; it would end on December 31, 1976. Final Congressional action came quickly. On October 12, the House approved the conference report 265 to 110; the Senate followed the next day by a vote of 59 to 19.

On October 20, President Nixon joined several hundred state, county, and community officials in a bill signing ceremony at Independence Hall, Philadelphia. Making the connection between revenue sharing and the historic site for the signing, Nixon said,

> this New American Revolution is truly underway....
>
> The American people are fed up with government that doesn't deliver. Revenue sharing can help State and local government deliver again, closing the gap between promise and performance.
>
> Revenue sharing will give these hard-pressed governments the dollars they need so badly. But just as importantly, it will give them the freedom they need to use those dollars as effectively as possible.
>
> Under revenue sharing, more decisions will be made at the scene of the action—and this means that more people can have a piece of the action. By multiplying the centers of effective power in our country we will be multiplying the opportunities for involvement and influence by individual citizens.[28]

The combination of Independence Hall and rhetoric gave revenue sharing a heady start.

CHAPTER VII

Implementation:
Problems and Issues

The implementation of public policy is not a popular field of political inquiry and research. Once policy is enacted there is frequently a fading of interest, as the political conflicts of the legislative process recede and are replaced by the less stirring matters of establishing an administrative bureaucracy, writing regulations and guidelines, and processing applications. The implementation of revenue sharing was generally routine, but there were a few significant departures from "normal."

A major difference was in the federal implementation mechanism itself. A new, fully funded $30 billion federal grant program would customarily have provided the impetus for a massive new bureaucratic structure or caused the major reorganization of an existing bureaucracy. This was not the case for tax sharing, which contemplated, as an integral part of the new policy, that most of the policy decisions and implementation responsibilities would be exercised by state and local officials. Revenue sharing funds were to be distributed automatically four times a year; thus, there were not thousands of applications to be processed or the requirements for state and local plan submittal before the money could be distributed. Without these, there were no massive administrative manuals or extensive forms to be developed. And, even though the law established spending categories, these were so broad that little difficulty was anticipated in gaining compliance. If any areas were to be subjected to close scrutiny, it would be to assure that the shared funds were not used as matching funds for other federal grants and that the money would not be used for racially segregated programs, an early concern of civil rights groups. Consequently, the only new structure was a small unit of the Treasury Department charged with writing and administering minimal regulations, servicing complaints, adjusting allocation formulas, and overseeing the reporting process established in the law. The Office of Revenue Sharing (ORS) had less than 50 people. The ease of implementing the law was shown by the fact that on December 8, just seven weeks after Nixon signed the law, the first checks, totalling $2.65 billion, were in the mail. It was largely a self-executing policy at the federal level.

Implementation of public policy is, however, more than a matter of routine administration. The results must be evaluated against expectations. The revenue sharing act itself did not carry with it a statement of policy goals, but it clearly had created some general expectations:

(1) The new money would bring some fiscal relief to state and local governments. Implicit in this was that tax sharing was to be in addition to existing grant aid, as stated on several occasions by the Nixon administration.

(2) In inserting a "need" factor into the distribution formula, Congress anticipated that tax sharing would have some equalization effect, giving greater benefits to the poorer areas than to richer ones.

(3) Revenue sharing would foster the decentralization of de-

cision making, granting greater policy authority over the use of federally-raised money to state and local officials. Concomitant with decentralized decision making was the view that this would result in more efficient use of resources by officials who were closer to the problem and who, therefore, could deal with local problems more effectively.

Since the first revenue sharing checks were not distributed until late 1972, it is too early as of this writing to assess conclusively the relationship between expectations and results, but early experience does provide some initial insights and raise issues for subsequent study.

SUBSTITUTION ISSUE REVIVED

The closing weeks of Congress, in the summer and fall of 1972, had been politically charged by a dispute between the President and Congress over the need to control the level of federal spending. Large deficits had been characteristic of the federal budget since the late 1960's, but the issue was revived in 1972 and became entwined in the election campaign. Nixon accused the Congress of "excessive" and "irresponsible" spending and said that unless some ceilings were put on spending, "Congressional" tax increases would be necessary. The President wanted a $250 billion limit on spending for fiscal year 1973 and asked for the authority to make selective program reductions. That is, he wanted Congress to permit him to pick and choose among federal programs for spending cutbacks. Congress itself was split on its response. The House passed a bill generally conforming to Nixon's request, but the Senate rejected granting such authority to the President. Opposition was based on the argument that this would, in effect, be granting the Chief Executive an item veto on appropriations, a power that had been deliberately denied the President in the past. Secondly, it was feared that the reductions would be applied primarily to various social welfare programs, rather than to such budget areas as defense and space. While the dispute was unresolved legislatively, it was clear that the Nixon administration had taken a strong position on controlling the budget and that this policy would be carried over to its second term.

Within days of his election victory, Nixon reaffirmed this position and gave his first indication of where he intended to make budget cutbacks. In a newspaper interview given before the election but not published until after it, Nixon said,

> What we have to realize is that many of the solutions of the 1960's were massive failures. They threw money at the problems and for the most part they have failed and we are going to shuck off those programs and trim down those programs that have proved simply to be failures.[1]

It was a clear signal that many of the Great Society programs aimed at solving problems of the cities were in trouble and faced likely reductions in the FY 74 budget being assembled at that time.

The President's interview statement was the major concern at a meeting of the National League of Cities held in Indianapolis, Indiana, in late November. At the meeting local officials expressed their concern that revenue sharing was, despite all assurances to the contrary, going to become a substitute for other grant programs. Thomas Bradley, Democratic City Councilman of Los Angeles, praised the new revenue sharing program but said,

> It is no substitute for other strong and continuous federal support to American cities in such programs as urban renewal, Model Cities and antipoverty. If, indeed, revenue sharing has become a device to shift $5 billion to cities and then say you spend the money to handle local problems according to your priorities, it would be the major domestic disaster of the 20th century.[2]

Deputy Undersecretary of the Treasury James Smith, an active Administration lobbyist for revenue sharing when it was being considered by Congress, was at the meeting and explained to the mayors some of the details of implementing the program, but he did not answer questions on whether revenue sharing was to be used as a substitute for other grant programs.

The NLC members, responding to Nixon and reminding the President that his Administration and Congress had made a commitment that grants would not be reduced because of revenue sharing, issued a "sense of the convention" statement: "Any reform of the federal aid system that diminished the funding already available to meet pressing human needs is simply a pretext for solving federal fiscal problems."[3] the convention also passed a formal urging the President and Congress to provide revenue sharing funds and, at the same time, to expand current grants.

It was not long before the Administration gave firm evidence that it intended to make major reductions in federal grants. Within weeks of the election, it was announced that the Administration would withhold the spending of $6 billion of the $11 billion Congress had approved for sewage treatment grants for fiscal years 1973 and 1974. Over the Christmas holidays, the Department of Agriculture notified the states that it intended to end two rural conservation programs that distributed more than $200 million a year in rural areas. The two programs chosen were the Rural Environmental Assistance Program, dating back to the mid-1930's, and the Water Bank program, enacted in 1971. It was a carefully considered announcement and made two points: first, the Administration was not adopting an anticity policy—the rural areas as well as the cities were going to be cut back; secondly, it was not an anti-Great Society policy—a program from the New Deal and one enacted during Nixon's own Administration were to be ended. The next blow did fall on the cities when, in early January, George Romney, Secretary of Housing and Urban Development, announced an eighteen-month freeze on all housing subsidies.

The policy of grant cutbacks was officially announced by Nixon in his budget message, sent to Congress in late January. Referring to the failure of many programs, Nixon said,

> The seeds of those failures were sown in the 1960's when the "do something, do anything" pressure for Federal panaceas led to the establishment of scores of well-intended social programs too often poorly conceived and hastily put together. . . . [this] budget proposes to reform those programs that can be made productive and to terminate those that were poorly conceived.[4]

The President's budget proposed a $268.7 billion spending program for fiscal year 1974. By reducing or terminating more than 100 programs, the Administration expected to save $6.5 billion in actual spending during fiscal 1973, an additional $16.9 billion in fiscal 1974, and $21.7 billion more in fiscal 1975. Among the programs to be terminated were the community action portion of the antipoverty program and the grant and loan programs of the Economic Development Administration. Nixon also announced plans to phase out local mental health programs and reduce farm subsidies. In addition, the President said he intended to renew his request to consolidate seventy federal grants into four special revenue sharing programs, education, law enforcement, manpower training, and urban development.*

The President said he was making the reductions and terminations to eliminate programs that had failed to work, but it was also evident that the idea of using revenue sharing funds as a substitute for some of these grants was contemplated. In refering to an end of funds for community action projects, the budget said, "In addition to private funds, State and local government may, of course, use general and special revenue sharing funds for these purposes."[5] This was clearly the language of a policy of substitution.

It was this sequence of events and the consequent belief that the Administration had deceived the mayors about revenue sharing as additional money that led to bitter criticism of the Administration during Senate hearings on the New Federalism held by Muskie in February 1973.[6] There, within three months of its first check-mailing, tax sharing was labeled a "Trojan horse," a "cruel hoax,"

*Nixon did not renew his requests for Rural Development and Transportation Special Revenue Sharing, because of heavy political resistance from Congress and various interest groups. Near the end of the first session of the 93rd Congress (December 1973), the manpower consolidation was approved by Congress in exchange for Nixon's acceptance of a Democratic-sponsored public employment grant program. Progress was being made for consolidation of some urban programs, but there were major differences between the Nixon and the Democratic approaches; prospects for major education and law enforcement consolidations were not as bright as for urban programs.

a "gigantic double-cross," by the same mayors who had spoken out so strongly and lobbied in behalf of revenue sharing during 1971 and 1972. However, despite this apparent surprise on the part of the mayors, the political and legislative history of tax sharing had carried indications throughout that the idea of sharing as a substitute for categorical grants had not disappeared from serious consideration in key policy-making places.

By late 1973, many of the Presidential initiatives to cut back programs and impound funds had been diverted by court decisions and by a reassertion of Congressional power, largely resulting from the Watergate affair. When Nixon submitted his FY 1975 budget to Congress in February 1974, he showed a more conciliatory attitude than he had a year earlier, but there was still clear evidence that he intended to pursue a policy of liquidating or consolidating some categorical programs and leveling off or reducing the spending on others.[7] He would, in his budget, dismantle the Office of Economic Opportunity and terminate the community action programs, end the Hill-Burton hospital construction grants, phase out community health centers, allot only $4 billion of the $7 billion that had been provided for construction of water pollution control facilities, and continue the freeze on nearly all housing subsidy programs.

The President's program for FY 1975 also renewed some of the tensions between state and city officials with its proposals for increasing the state share of funds for drug abuse control and comprehensive areawide planning and for converting the local-oriented categorical programs of the Economic Development Administration into a broad purpose grant to state governments.[8]

The developments between November 1972 and the spring of 1974 altered the perceptions of revenue sharing held by the nation's mayors and governors and convinced some Congressmen long suspicious of revenue sharing that their doubts had been well founded. The mayors, while they still supported revenue sharing and no strings money, had begun to view with great concern the parallel actions being taken to terminate or reduce other local aid programs. They also had become sensitized to some implications of the decentralizing thrust of New Federalism. The mayors clearly supported the general principle of decentralization, which promised to put more decision-making responsibility into their hands, but it was becoming apparent that New Federalism also meant some of their funds shifted up to the state level, a development which they firmly opposed.

The happenings of the first year and a half of implementation are likely to greatly influence future consideration of revenue sharing when it expires in 1976. The Nixon policy of budget cuts and program terminations was not, however, the only significant event during this time. Another problem area was the allocation of money.

EQUALIZATION: DATA EFFECTS

The House and Senate Committees, with the aid of Treasury Department computers, had sought to establish allocation formulas that gave some distribution advantage to areas with weak economic bases. One element in the equalization effort was the basing of distributions partially on need, as measured by relative per capita income. Another was the tax effort factor, designed to aid the central cities by weighting the allocations toward those areas with high taxes and low income levels. In the House, this redistribution bias had been diluted by inclusion of the urbanized population criterion, which tended to favor the rapidly growing suburban areas. The Senate version of the local distribution formula, the one finally adopted, by eliminating the urbanization factor and thus giving more weight to relative income and tax effort, had the net effect of again biasing the allocations toward the poorer central cities and rural areas. In short, the final formulas reflected an effort on the part of lawmakers to combine both need and political acceptability

As the two committees worked on the formulas, extensive computer runs were made showing how much each state, each county, and each major municipality would receive. The final committee reports of both House and Senate contained a detailed listing of the estimated amounts these jurisdictions would receive under the respective formulas. Despite the fact that these were estimated allocations, when the bill was signed into law many governors, county officials, city managers, and mayors thought they were assured a specified amount. Some difficulties quickly appeared.

Just before the first checks were to be mailed in early December, the Treasury Department reported that there would be major dollar differences from the estimates for many state and local governments. About 6,000 communities would receive an amount 50 percent or more below previous estimates. Another 7,000 would receive 50 percent or more above the early estimates. The problem was in the data used in calculating the actual distributions. The Congressional estimates had been based in part on unrefined data from the 1970 population census and in part on 1967 tax collection data. Congress had provided in the law that the Secretary of the Treasury should use later statistics in applying the allocation formulas. Therefore, in making its first allocation schedule, the Department used the final reports of the 1970 population census and had a special survey made by the Census Bureau to update the state and local tax data to 1971. The result of using this later tax information was that the nation's faster growing areas benefited most while the older areas suffered the most losses. Generally speaking, the metropolitan suburbs were the biggest gainers. Thus, in the first distribution, some of the equalization effect was lost by the use of later data. Moreover, the data adjustment was not a one-time change.

As part of its operating procedures, the Treasury Department intended to adjust the allocations annually over the life of the program.[9] That is, each year the Department would recompute the allocations and adjust all distributions upward or downward as necessary. Annual adjustments would seem to be a neutral decision, in that the results attained would assure that the money continued to be distributed in accordance with general Congressional expectations. The problem was, however, that data collections systems existing at the time the program got under way did not permit all elements of the data base to be updated. The major adjustment that the Treasury Department made at the outset was for changes in the tax collections of governmental units, thus altering the tax effort portion of the three-part formula. Estimates of population changes in the states were subsequently made by the Census Bureau, but not changes in local population, although efforts were being made to update population data for the larger local units. The per capita income data would continue to come from the 1970 census because there were no procedures available to make reliable estimates of income changes. There are major implications to such uneven adjustment of the data base.

As the suburbs continue to grow in population, they are also likely to have increased tax collections, simply because there will be more people paying taxes. If the income data do not change, a likely possibility is that many suburban areas will show a greater tax effort, when in fact the tax burdens on the residents have not changed. For example, in fiscal 1974 a suburb may report adjusted tax collections of $1 million;* the aggregate income for the community from the census report is $6 million. The tax effort would be $1 million divided by $6 million or .166. Let us say that over the next three years the population of the suburb increases because of new subdivisions, and tax collections rise by $200,000, even though the tax rate does not change. Now the same suburb would report tax collections of $1,200,000; the aggregate income figure would remain the same. The tax effort calculation now becomes 1,200,000 divided by the same $6 million, or .2. By simple population growth, this suburb appears to be making a greater tax effort when, in fact, the tax burdens are no greater. A central city, on the other

---

*"Adjusted" taxes excluded revenues allocated to educational expenditures.

hand, which is more likely to have a static or declining population, can only have a higher tax effort index by actual increase of its tax burden. The net effect over a period of years may be that a greater proportion of revenue sharing funds will go to the expanding, better off suburbs at the expense of the poorer communities. (Another complicating factor in achieving some of the intended equalization effect is an apparent 7.7 percent undercount of the Black population in the 1970 census, having particularly adverse implications for those large cities with concentrations of Blacks.)

The critical point in the readjustment process seems to be the absence of a means for adjusting per capita income, which is tied to the 1970 census. Updating of this factor would affect the relative income criterion in ways that would aid the poorer areas, as incomes in such communities tend to increase at a slower rate than in the expanding suburban areas. Since grant allocation formulas are designed with a bias of some kind, a change in the data base that affects only parts of a formula will result in alteration of the initial bias. Members of the Ways and Means and Finance Committees were aware of these data difficulties and the problems of adjustment, but concluded it was better to allow the distributions of money to follow the patterns of national growth than to freeze the allocations to old data and have a kind of "rotten borough" revenue sharing system.

In sum, the planned regular adjustments of the data base appear to lead to two results. First, loss of some of the equalization effect. Revenue sharing, aimed partially at helping "poor governments," seems likely to direct larger proportions of the money to the "not so poor governments." Second, compounding of the uncertainty experienced by some local officials about revenue sharing money, very possibly leading to greater difficulty when the future of the program comes to be decided. Some community decisions on spending revenue sharing money have already been influenced by the fact that the program is not guaranteed beyond five years, and governments are, therefore, reluctant to tie the money to certain types of spending. For some communities, this form of uncertainty will be heightened by their inability to rely on a given amount of money even during the life of the program. Thus, even seemingly mechanical matters such as distribution formulas and uses of demographic and financial data have important political impacts on present and future policy decisions and evaluations.

REDISTRIBUTION: DECISIONAL EFFECTS

One early and basic objection to revenue sharing sprang from the fear that unearmarked federal funds going to state and local officials would be wasted or spent primarily to meet the demands of the politically and economically advantaged. The revenue sharing law did nothing to eliminate such concerns, and the redistributive and nonredistributive allocation decisions of state and local officials have become a focal point in evaluating the impact of the program.

In Chapter I the point was made that the federal government, through the progressive income tax, has an economic redistribution function, and it was suggested there that revenue sharing, as a mechanism for resource allocations, should be evaluated in terms of this function. To what extent is it reasonable and desirable that state and local governments use these redistributive funds for redistributive purposes, or should there be any redistributive expectation at all?

The law permits state governments to use revenue sharing funds for any purpose except as matching funds for federal grants. Local officials, however, are restricted in their use of the money for operating and maintenance expenditures to specified categories, but they are permitted to use the funds for any capital expenditure. It should also be recalled that with the elimination of any local maintenance of effort requirement, revenue sharing money became, in effect, unrestricted money in the overall budget-making process.

Evaluation of local decision making on the basis of a

redistributive-nonredistributive criterion, as defined in Chapter I, requires some elaborate model building. Certainly it is more than a simple dichotomy between the "capital" and "operating and maintenance" categories and subcategories mandated by the law. Capital expenditures could be made for a health clinic for the community's poor, a redistributive decision; a nonredistributive capital expenditure might be a new storm drain system in the downtown business area.

Similarly, operating and maintenance expenditures may also have either type of distribution effect. In many cases, such expenditures will go for salary increases or, in some instances, the community's contribution to public employee retirement systems. These tend to be nonredistributive decisions and may be the local response to the pressure of strong public employee organizations. (It is easy to see why education was excluded as an eligible operating and maintenance category, for powerful teacher unions would have added to such pressures on local governments.) A redistributive purpose might be the use of funds to reduce the local bus fare for the elderly, many of whom have very low incomes. There is a good chance that a significant proportion of elderly bus riders will have low incomes and thus enjoy the redistributive advantages of such subsidies. At the same time, simply assigning funds to programs for the elderly might be deceptive in its impact. One community used revenue sharing money to reduce the golf green fees for retired persons, a use that is not likely to be as redistributive in its effects.

There is also an evaluation problem in the use of revenue sharing funds to reduce or avoid increases in the property tax, a purpose Nixon and many others frequently stated when the legislation was being considered in Congress. Such use may also be redistributive or nonredistributive. Since the property tax is a regressive tax, any relief for low-income homeowners may have some redistributive effect. At the same time, general property tax relief extends the same benefits to the upper income homeowners, where such relief will be nonredistributive. Therefore, to evaluate the use of revenue sharing funds for property tax relief by a redistributive-nonredistributive criterion requires a distinction between general tax relief and the easing of the property tax burden on an income scale. In either case, determination of a direct relationship between a community's receipt of revenue sharing funds and the impact on property tax rates is very difficult to establish. The question in any community would be: What would the property tax rate have been if we had not received the revenue sharing money? The answer is problematic, since without the revenue sharing money some of the expenditures might not have been made. Nevertheless, the point remains that any analysis of the relationships between revenue sharing funds and local property taxes should include redistributive-nonredistributive consideration.

Another distribution consideration arises in the issue of federal cutbacks in some aid programs and the substitution of revenue sharing funds for categorical grants. Because of these threatened and real reductions, some communities have used, or expect to use, part of their revenue sharing money to replace the loss of antipoverty, Model City, or other social welfare funds. Local officials may be forced into redistributive decisions by actions at the federal level, but since the money would only be a substitute for reduced federal redistributive aid, there would be no additive effect.

Revenue sharing is a recent policy innovation, so it is premature to draw any conclusions about the impact of the program. However, several studies have been made that yield some initial information on general spending decisions, although they provide little data on which to base redistributive-nonredistributive analysis.

An early survey of the fifty states and more than seven hundred units of local government receiving funds found that capital expenditures constituted the leading use local officials intended to make of initial allocations.[10] This survey, made for ORS by Technology Management Incorporated (TMI), reported 72 percent of the 574 communities that responded to the survey ranked capital expenditures in their top three spending choices. This was followed by public safety operating and maintenance expenditures (57 percent of the respondents) and environmental protection operations and maintenance (35 percent). At the state level, the U.S. General Accounting Office (GAO), in another early study, reported that of the $957.9 million it had identified going for specific uses, 58 percent had been authorized or planned for education expenditures and 39 percent had been designated for capital expenditures, mainly construction and land acquisition.[11]

The TMI study noted several reasons given for the local preference for capital expenditures. First was the neglect that capital improvements and acquisitions had experienced in recent years because of restrictions on available funds and the public reaction against bond issues for capital outlays. But there was also the clear feeling that the language of the law and the limited duration of the program made it easier to spend the money on capital programs than on operations and maintenance, indicating the federal policy itself biased the decision making toward capital expenditures. There was some reluctance among state and local decision makers to commit tax sharing funds to operating expenses and then find them cut off at the end of the program. It was perceived as being easier to put the money into one-time capital expenditures than to spend it on program operations, where it would be far more difficult to reduce spending later.

The TMI study did not break down the capital expenditures, but there were subcategories within the operating and maintenance category. As noted above, public safety (generally, police and fire protection) and environmental protection were the two leading preferences of local officials. These were followed by public transportation (31 percent of the respondents), recreation (20 percent), and health (19 percent). The lowest priority areas for local government were social services (8 percent) and libraries (6 percent). Of the 35 responding state governments, five said they expected to use funds for "social development." At the bottom of the state list of priorities were community development and economic development, with none of the responding states having plans for such expenditures. While providing some useful data on intended expenditures, this report has two important limitations. First, the statistics are percentages of responding units of government and thus give no indications of dollar amounts. Second, the data provide little insight for redistributive-nonredistributive analysis, although it should be noted that the proportion of state and local governments planning to spend funds on social services or social development was low.

A second study, published by ORS in March 1974, examined the actual use of general revenue sharing funds through June 30, 1973.[12] This study, made for ORS by David A. Caputo and Richard L. Cole, reported that, in making actual expenditure decisions, state and local officials were using a larger proportion of the money for operating and maintenance expenditures than had been anticipated.

> The implication appears to be that many units of government planned to expend a higher proportion of their funds for capital expenditures but had not been able to do so because of the pressing demand of daily operating and maintenance needs.[13]

Of the $2.8 billion that had been actually expended by mid-1973, 67 percent went for operating and maintenance expenses, with 33 percent allocated to capital projects. Only county governments spent more than half of their funds on capital expenditures, probably, the report noted, a reflection of functional responsibilities.

The TMI and Caputo-Cole studies indicated different patterns in the division between capital and operating and maintenance expenditures, but they did show considerable similarity in the specific functional areas that were given high priority. The TMI study found public safety, environmental protection, and public transportation to be the three categories most frequently preferred by local decision makers. Caputo and Cole found these same three categories receiving 72 percent of the money spent by cities, 54

TABLE VI

Reported Actual Use of General Revenue Sharing:
All Units of Government—1/1/72-6/30/73* (in millions of dollars)

Category	Operating and Maintenance			Capital		Total	Total Funds
	Amount	Category	New Services	Amount	Category		
Public Safety	$496.4	76%	8%	$158.8	24%	$655.2	23%
Environmental Protection Conservation	92.5	49%	16%	95.3	51%	187.8	7%
Public Transportation	183.8	44%	12%	233.1	56%	416.9	15%
Health	99.3	60%	8%	66.5	40%	165.8	6%
Recreation/Culture	35.6	31%	28%	81.1	69%	116.7	4%
Libraries	18.5	100%	14%	-0-	-0-	18.5	1%
Social Services for the Poor or Aged	88.1	100%	13%	-0-	-0-	88.1	3%
Financial Administration	69.9	100%	25%	-0-	-0-	69.9	2%
Education	643.0	94%	39%	44.2	6%	687.2	24%
Multi-Purpose/General Government	-0-	-0-	-0-	183.7	100%	183.7	6%
Social Development	-0-	-0-	-0-	12.9	100%	12.9	.5%
Housing/Community Development	-0-	-0-	-0-	26.0	100%	26.0	1%
Economic Development	-0-	-0-	-0-	11.6	100%	11.6	.5%
Other	149.8	84%	3%	27.8	16%	177.6	6%
Totals	$1876.9	67%	20%	$941.0	33%	$2817.9	100%**

All Units: Total Amount Disbursed = $6620.7; Total Amount Expended = $2817.9; Percent Expended = 42.5

*Note: In this and the following tables, totals are calculated on total amounts of revenue sharing funds disbursed and total amounts expended as reported in the analyzed reports. The totals do not include earned interest on revenue sharing disbursements nor do they include estimates for the reports not yet available when these analyses were made. In the tables which follow, totals may not always equal one another due to rounding procedures and errors.

**Percents do not total 100% because of rounding.

Source: U.S., Department of the Treasury, Office of Revenue Sharing, Revenue Sharing: The First Actual Use Reports (Washington: U.S. Government Printing Office, 1974), pp.4-5.

percent for counties, and 74 percent for township governments. In redistributive-nonredistributive terms, it is unlikely that public safety and environmental protection would have a significant redistributive impact; public transportation is a greater possibility, but more information on specific uses would be necessary for any reasonable conclusions to be made. At the state level, Caputo and Cole reported 65 percent of the earmarked funds going for education, a finding similar to the GAO study.

While the problem of determining redistributive-nonredistributive uses within the various categories remained, the Caputo-Cole study did give a clearer indication of actual expenditures for social services. During the first 18 months of the program, only $88.1 million or 3 percent was earmarked for social services for the poor or aged, including both capital and operating and maintenance expenditures. Of that $88.1 million, $61.2 million was spent by state governments. Among local governments there were some slight variations in the percentages spent for such services, the variations being related to size: counties with 250,000 or more population spent 5 percent of their funds on social services; those with 25,000 to 249,000 spent 3 percent; those below 25,000 spent 1 percent. While the county data suggested that the more populous counties tended to spend more on social services, it should be noted that the amounts of money involved were very small. The 124 counties in the largest category spent only a total of $12.8 milllion on social services. Among the cities the percentage was about the same, 1 to 2 percent, regardless of size.

In another finding, Caputo and Cole reported that 44 percent of all units of government felt that the revenue sharing money had reduced or helped avoid tax increases; 27 percent believed there was no effect on taxes; the remainder indicated that it was too early to predict the impact of the new money on taxes.[14] About twenty state governments felt there would be no effect on state taxes, presumably because the amount of revenue sharing funds going to the state represented only a very small percentage of the state budget.

TABLE VII

Reported Actual Use of General Revenue Sharing: by Type of Local Government (in millions of dollars)

| | Counties (N = 2,876) | | | | | Cities (N = 15,785) | | | | |
| | Operating and Maintenance | | Capital | | Total Funds | Operating and Maintenance | | Capital | | Total Funds |
Category	Amount	Category	Amount	Category		Amount	Category	Amount	Category	
Public Safety	$99.9	67%	$49.7	33%	23%	$343.0	79%	$91.0	21%	44%
Environmental Protection/Conservation	16.6	42%	23.4	59%	6%	65.8	52%	60.2	48%	13%
Public Transportation	61.0	38%	100.5	62%	25%	55.6	37%	93.1	63%	15%
Health	46.6	60%	31.0	40%	12%	21.0	42%	29.3	58%	5%
Recreation/Culture	8.6	29%	20.8	71%	5%	22.8	30%	53.8	70%	8%
Libraries	6.3	100%	-0-	-0-	1%	10.4	100%	-0-	-0-	1%
Social Services for the Poor or Aged	17.5	100%	-0-	-0-	2%	11.7	100%	-0-	-0-	1%
Financial Administration	30.3	100%	-0-	-0-	5%	16.0	100%	-0-	-0-	2%
Education*	-0-	-0-	16.3	100%	2%	-0-	-0-	4.7	100%	-0-
Multi-Purpose/General Government*	-0-	-0-	97.6	100%	15%	-0-	-0-	65.7	100%	7%
Social Development*	-0-	-0-	6.0	100%	1%	-0-	-0-	3.1	100%	-0-
Housing/Community Development*	-0-	-0-	8.3	100%	1%	-0-	-0-	14.4	100%	2%
Economic Development*	-0-	-0-	1.8	100%	-0-	-0-	-0-	7.3	100%	1%
Other*	-0-	-0-	12.5	100%	2%	-0-	-0-	8.6	100%	1%
Totals	$286.8	44%	$367.9	56%	100%	$546.3	56%	$431.2	44%	100%

Counties: Total Amount Disbursed $1688.8
Total Amount Expended $654.7
Percent Expended 38.8

Cities: Total Amount Disbursed $2357.8
Total Amount Expended $977.5
Percent Expended 41.5

TABLE VII CONTINUED

	Townships					Indian Tribes and Alaskan Native Villages				
Public Safety	$38.3	74%	$13.2	26%	33%	$.2	100%	-0-	-0-	12%
Environmental Protection/Conservation	8.7	60%	5.7	40%	9%	.1	100%	-0-	-0-	6%
Public Transportation	21.7	43%	29.2	57%	32%	.1	50%	.1	50%	12%
Health	3.6	51%	3.5	49%	4%	.2	67%	.1	33%	18%
Recreation/Culture	2.6	41%	4.2	59%	4%	.1	50%	.1	50%	12%
Libraries	1.7	100%	-0-	-0-	1%	-0-	-0-	-0-	-0-	-0-
Social Services for the Poor or Aged	1.3	100%	-0-	-0-	1%	.1	100%	-0-	-0-	6%
Financial Administration	5.0	100%	-0-	-0-	3%	.2	100%	-0-	-0-	12%
Education*	-0-	-0-	1.9	100%	1%	-0-	-0-	-0-	-0-	-0-
Multi-Purpose General Government*	-0-	-0-	14.3	100%	9%	-0-	-0-	.2	100%	12%
Social Development*	-0-	-0-	.1	100%	-0-	-0-	-0-	-0-	-0-	-0-
Housing/Community Development*	-0-	-0-	2.1	100%	1%	-0-	-0-	.1	100%	6%
Economic Development*	-0-	-0-	.1	100%	-0-	-0-	-0-	.1	100%	6%
Other*	-0-	-0-	3.6	100%	2%	-0-	-0-	-0-	-0-	-0-
Totals	$82.9	52%	$77.9	48%	100%	$1.0	59%	$.7	51%	102%**

Townships:

Total Amount Disbursed	$325.4
Total Amount Expended	$160.8
Percent Expended	49.4

Indian Tribes and Alaskan Native Villages:

Total Amount Disbursed	$7.9
Total Amount Expended	$1.7
Percent Expended	21.5

*These are not allowable categories of operating and maintenance expenditure for local governments: they are allowable for ordinary and necessary capital expenditures.

**Percents do not all total 100 percent because of rounding.

Source: *Revenue Sharing First Actual Use Report*, pp.10-13.

As shown by the TMI, GAO, and Caputo-Cole studies, one difficulty in evaluating decentralized decision making by a redistributive-nonredistributive criterion is the limited content of the state and local reports on planned and actual expenditures. ORS has designed a simple one-page reporting form carrying the categories and subcategories of capital and operating and maintenance expenditures. This simplified form complies with the general thrust of revenue sharing to impose as few reporting burdens as possible on state and local governments, but it will not greatly aid redistributive-nonredistributive analysis. For this, much more precise expenditure information is needed, and it must be measured against the characteristics of individual communities in terms of their resources and their social and economic problems and needs. A community with severe income, housing, and health problems that develops a record of continuously disproportionate nonredistributive decisions is likely to influence (or confirm) citizen attitudes about revenue sharing and the local political system. The TMI and Caputo-Cole studies do include such variables as the size of the community, region, and relative tax effort, but additional variables are needed for evaluation of revenue sharing impacts. Among them would be socio-economic indicators, refined expenditure categories, and political and budgetary process variables.

Integrally related to an analysis of policy impact is the extent of public participation in local decisions on how revenue sharing money will be spent. One of the philosophic premises for revenue sharing was that decentralization of policy making was desirable because the state and local governments are closer to the people, and citizens thus could be expected to have a greater say in the use of the tax sharing money than they have when the money comes through federal bureaucrats. To encourage citizen interest, the final revenue sharing legislation included a provision requiring all recipient governments to publicize both planned and actual uses of the funds in a general circulation newspaper. It was an-

TABLE VIII

Reported Actual Use of General Revenue Sharing:
State Government—12/31/72—6/30/73 (in millions of dollars)

Category	Operating and Maintenance			Capital		Total	Total Funds
	Amount	Category	New Services	Amount	Category	Total	Total Funds
Public Safety	$15.1	76%	2%	$4.9	24%	$20.0	2%
Environmental Protection/Conservation	1.3	18%	7%	6.1	82%	7.4	1%
Public Transportation	45.5	82%	-0-	10.1	18%	55.6	5%
Health	28.0	91%	-0-	2.7	9%	30.7	3%
Recreation/Culture	1.4	38%	-0-	2.3	62%	3.7	-0-
Libraries*	-0-	-0-	-0-	-0-	-0-	-0-	-0-
Social Services for the Poor or Aged	57.5	94%	7%	3.7	6%	61.2	6%
Financial Administration	18.5	100%	48%	-0-	-0-	18.5	2%
Education	643.0	97%	39%	21.3	3%	664.3	65%
Multi-Purpose/General Government	-0-	-0-	-0-	5.9	100%	5.9	1%
Housing/Community Development	-0-	-0-	-0-	1.1	100%	1.1	-0-
Economic Development	-0-	-0-	-0-	2.2	100%	2.2	-0-
Other	148.8	98%	3%	3.1	2%	151.9	15%
Totals	$959.1	94%	28%	$63.4	6%	$1022.5	100%

State Governments: Total Amount Disbursed = $2256.0; Total Amount Expended = $1022.5; Percent Expended = 45.3

*"Libraries" was not identified as a separate reporting category on the State Actual Use Report; any expenditures for Libraries would have been included in the "Other" category.

Source: Revenue Sharing First Actual Use Report, pp. 8-9.

ticipated that such publicity would assist individual and group access to the decision-making process and therefore influence the use of revenue sharing money. The issue of a mechanism to aid citizen participation was first raised by Chairman Long during Senate Finance Committee consideration of the legislation. He proposed that spending plans be submitted to a public referendum for approval. Local officials felt this would be an unworkable provision, so Long compromised and accepted the newspaper publicity approach.

The TMI report found that 20 percent of the communities responding to the survey had more citizen participation in tax sharing decision making than in other local budget decisions.[15] Generally, this was found in the more populous areas. Thirty-nine percent of the communities said they expected more participation in the future as more publicity is given to planned local uses of the money. At the state level, only 9 percent of the responses noted increases in public participation, and only 14 percent expected an increase in the future. The low state expectation was linked to the fact that revenue sharing represents a very small percentage of a state government's total budget and therefore is much less visible to the public.

The study drew several important conclusions about public participation. First, the increase in such participation appeared to result from the initiatives made by local officials to encourage such participation. Second, because decision making on revenue sharing money has been integrated into the regular budgetary process, it would be unusual if there were a marked increase in public participation over that normally found in the budgeting process. Third, the increase in participation is partially attributable to the "novelty of the program and the national publicity given the initial funds distribution. Public interest due to this activity could be expected to diminish over time."[16]

It is important to reemphasize that the data of the early studies were too preliminary to permit any firm conclusions about future decision making at the state and local levels. However, the political history of the program, the expectations generated, and the initial results do suggest the kinds of questions that need to be asked about the program. Clearly a central question concerns the issue of policy decentralization and the impact such decision making has on state and local problem solving.

A Future View

The making of public policy is a subject that has long fascinated observers and students of the American political process. Everyone has his private view of what he would like to see done to deal with national problems, whether it be doing more or doing less. Regardless of what this private view may be, there is a commonly shared image of how we proceed with the process of identifying problems, devising a policy response, and putting policy into effect. This image has variously been referred to as "gradualism," "incrementalism," or by more jargonized terms such as "successive limited comparisons." But, whatever the term, what it roughly means is that policy making in this country is a building block approach, flowing from the political interplay between Congress, the President, the bureaucracy, interest groups, and the invisible hand of national consensus. We take a problem, adopt a politically acceptable but limited approach to its solution, and then, step by step, we begin to push the margins of the policy outward, doing a bit more this year, perhaps a bit more the next. We are not given to quantum policy leaps or once-and-for-all solutions.

This has been the operating policy process in this country throughout most of its history and particularly during the past forty years, a process that has resulted in a panoply of federal programs that dealt with problems as they arose. To proponents it was "the foot in the door" approach; to opponents it was "creeping socialism." It has not been a very tidy system and has resulted in many problems of program duplication, overlap, and red tape. But it has also resulted in a conscious federally sponsored effort to cope with a myriad of problems that have surfaced over the years in the cities and in the countryside. It is at this juncture that revenue sharing, a product of this process, enters and poses questions, as this study points out, not only for the future of such programs but for the policy process itself.

Had revenue sharing been offered by the Nixon administration as the ultimate policy for repealing parts of the New Deal and much of the Great Society, the effort would certainly have failed. If ours is a system that does not permit sudden, dramatic great leaps forward, it is also a system that does not permit sudden, dramatic great leaps backward either. The political history of revenue sharing shows that when the point was raised the Nixon administration referred to revenue sharing as money to be added to existing categorical grants. But the political history also shows that in 1970 Nixon was considering the opposite—the possibility of cashing in all categorical grants and using the money for revenue sharing. It did not take long to discover that this was politically unfeasible and probably impossible at that time. Such a plan was too drastic; it was not incremental.

What evolved instead was an effort to develop a new national consensus that believes that the federal efforts to solve social problems have failed, that the national government has been inept and inefficient, that state and local bureaucracies can do a better job than the national bureaucracy. This consensus building was capped in Nixon's second term inaugural speech, when he told the American people that they must now ask not what the government can do for them, but what they can do for themselves.

Alone, this consensus manipulation would not be sufficient to unmake social policy. But it is the frame of mind necessary if the public is to accept a new policy approach, a policy of *decrementalism*. This policy operates in a reverse fashion from incrementalism. The latter is the process of expanding policy at the margins enough (either in additional money or in new programs) to keep most concerned groups reasonably satisfied. Decrementalism turns this around, shrinking selected policies at the margins by impoundments, phase outs, and terminations just enough to keep people from becoming outraged. However, decrementalism, while having budgetary implications for individual programs, is not basically a budgetary policy. Increases in total federal aid to state and local governments (due to growth in income support programs) may coexist with it. Fundamentally, it is a policy whereby the federal government gradually reduces its own policy role of defining and overseeing the resolution of particular social and economic problems and turns more and more decision making over to state and local officials, who use federal money as they see fit. Within this context, revenue sharing, as implemented by the Nixon administration, is seen by some of its opponents as the cutting edge of a new process not of incremental policy making, but of incremental policy unmaking. The FY 1974 and 1975 budgets were seen to confirm this view.

This process of policy decrementalism has major implications for the disadvantaged groups. Much federal aid policy since the New Deal had been developed from two basic assumptions about state and local governments: their fiscal incapacity to deal with many social and economic problems, and their unwillingness to undertake the task because of political and institutional biases. Revenue sharing may partially meet the fiscal problem, but it ignores the political and institutional obstacles that were among the factors originally considered in establishing many aid programs. Some programs have had disappointing results partially because of political and institutional problems at the local level of government (e.g., the concentration of public housing in central cities because of suburban resistance). Implicitly, decrementalism, as manifested in revenue sharing and other policies of the New Federalism, pretends that these problems have now disappeared and that all things have been rendered politically equal. They have not. Nevertheless, the disadvantaged groups are once again being asked to contend themselves with many of the same obstacles and biases that the federal government has found so resistant to change.

Supporters of revenue sharing, on the other hand, say that sharing is simply the substitution of one form of aid policy for another and not the retreat of the federal government from policy responsibilities.

This is where the political history of revenue sharing takes on added importance, because what is perceived as the major conflict ahead is not the fate of a particular program but the future of the entire intergovernmental policy process. The issues that have already arisen—the Nixon policies on grant eliminations and reductions, the data problems, and the state and local spending decisions—will greatly influence the political future of the program when it expires in 1976, another Presidential election year. But the early problems clearly do not mean that the chief elements of support for revenue sharing, the state and local officials, have become so disillusioned that they will no longer endorse the policy. It would take far greater problems than have arisen so far to divert these groups from their support for revenue sharing. If the state and local officials have a continuing philosophical posture toward federal aid, it is that they want as much money as they can get with as few strings as possible. Thus the future efforts of the state and local lobbyists are not likely to be in opposition to revenue sharing, but in favor of more sharing and legislative remedies for problem areas. The same, however, does not hold for some Congressional liberals, who are now convinced that revenue sharing, in its present form, will mean the ultimate dismantling of much of the federal policy role in the aid system. To the extent that this latter group is correct, either revenue sharing will be reshaped by the liberals to assure a redistributive impact with meaningful controls, or revenue sharing may once again find its chief support from the conservative elements of Congress.

Selected Bibliography

PUBLIC DOCUMENTS

Advisory Commission on Intergovernmental Relations. *Periodic Congressional Reassessment of Federal Grants-in-Aid to State and Local Governments.* Washington: U.S. Government Printing Office, 1961.
_____. *The Role of Equalization in Federal Grants.* Washington: U.S. Government Printing Office, 1964.
_____. *Fiscal Balance in the American Federal System.* Vols. I and II. Washington: U.S. Government Printing Office, 1967.
_____. *Eighth Annual Report.* Washington: U.S. Government Printing Office, 1967.
_____. *Ninth Annual Report.* Washington: U.S. Government Printing Office, 1968.
U.S., Commission on Intergovernmental Relations. *An Advisory Committee Report on Local Government.* Washington: U.S. Government Printing Office, 1955.
_____. *A Report to the President for Transmittal to the Congress.* Washington: U.S. Government Printing Office, 1955.
U.S., Comptroller General. *Revenue Sharing: Its Use by and Impact on State Governments.* Report to the Congress. Washington: General Accounting Office, Aug. 1973.
U.S., Congress, House and Senate Subcommittees on Intergovernmental Relations of the Committees on Government Operations. *Joint Hearings, Five-Year Record of the Advisory Commission on Intergovernmental Relations and Its Future Role.* 89th Cong., 1st Sess., 1965.
U.S., Congress, Joint Committee on Internal Revenue Taxation. *General Explanation of the State and Local Fiscal Assistance Act.* Feb. 12, 1973.
U.S., Congress, Subcommittee on Fiscal Policy of the Joint Economic Committee. *Hearings, Revenue Sharing and Its Alternatives: What Future for Fiscal Federalism?* 90th Cong., 1st Sess., 1967.
U.S., Department of the Treasury, Office of Revenue Sharing. *Preliminary Survey of General Revenue Sharing Recipient Governments* (unpublished report by Technology Management Inc.). June 19, 1973.
_____. *General Revenue Sharing: The First Actual Use Reports.* Washington: U.S. Government Printing Office, Mar. 1974.
U.S., House of Representatives, Committee on Interstate and Foreign

Commerce. *Comprehensive Health Planning and Public Health Services Amendments of 1966.* Rpt. No. 2271. 89th Cong., 2nd Sess., 1966.

U.S., House of Representatives, Committee on Education and Labor. *Elementary and Secondary Education Amendments of 1967.* Rpt. No. 188. 90th Cong., 1st Sess., 1967.

U.S., House of Representatives, Committee on Government Operations. *Hearings, Joint Funding Simplification.* 91st Cong., 1st Sess., 1969.

U.S., House of Representatives, Committee on Ways and Means. *Hearings, General Revenue Sharing.* Parts 1-8. 92nd Cong., 1st Sess., 1971.

———. *State and Local Fiscal Assistance Act of 1972.* Rpt. No. 1018, April 26, 1972. 92nd Cong., 2nd Sess., 1972.

U.S., Joint Federal-State Action Committee. *Report to the President of the United States and to the Chairman of the Governor's Conference.* Progress Rpt. No. 1. Washington: U.S. Government Printing Office, 1957.

———. *Final Report to the President of the United States and to the Chairman of the Governor's Conference.* Washington: U.S. Government Printing Office, 1960.

U.S., Senate, Committee on Finance. *Hearings, Revenue Sharing.* 92nd Cong., 2nd Sess., 1972.

———. *Revenue Sharing Act of 1972.* Rpt. No. 1050, Aug. 16, 1972. 92nd Cong., 2nd Sess., 1972.

———. *State and Local Fiscal Assistance Act of 1972.* Conference Report. Rpt. No. 1229, Sept. 26, 1972. 92nd Cong., 2nd Sess., 1972.

U.S., Senate, Subcommittee on Intergovernmental Relations of the Committee on Government Operations. *Hearings, Intergovernmental Revenue Act of 1971 and Related Legislation.* 92nd Cong., 1st Sess., 1971.

———. *Hearings, A New Federalism.* Parts I and II. 93rd Cong., 1st Sess., 1973.

U.S., *Weekly Compilation of Presidential Documents.* Vol. II, No. 11, and Vol. VIII, No. 43. Washington: U.S. Government Printing Office.

BOOKS

American Academy of Political and Social Science. "Intergovernmental Relations in the United States," *The Annals.* Philadelphia, 1965.

Anderson, William. *Intergovernmental Relations in Review.* Minneapolis: Univ. of Minnesota Press, 1960.

———. *The Nation and the States: Rivals or Partners?* Minneapolis: Univ. of Minnesota Press, 1955.

Bachrach, Peter, and Morton S. Baratz. *Power & Poverty: Theory and Practice.* New York: Oxford Univ. Press, 1970.

Binstock, Robert H., and Katherine Ely (eds.). *The Politics of the Powerless.* Cambridge, Mass.: Winthrop Pub., 1971.

Break, George F. *Intergovernmental Fiscal Relations in the United States.* Washington: Brookings Institution, 1967.

Campbell, Alan K. (ed.). *The States and the Urban Crisis.* Englewood Cliffs, N.J.: Prentice-Hall, 1970.

Clark, Jane Perry. *The Rise of a New Federalism.* Morningside Heights, N.Y.: Columbia Univ. Press, 1938.

Connery, Robert H., and Richard H. Leach. *The Federal Government and Metropolitan Areas.* Cambridge, Mass.: Harvard Univ. Press, 1960.

Cronin, Thomas E., and Sanford D. Greenberg (eds.). *The Presidential Advisory System.* New York: Harper & Row, 1969.

Ecker-Racz, L. L. *The Politics and Economics of State-Local Finance.* Englewood Cliffs, N.J.: Prentice-Hall, 1970.

Elazar, Daniel J. *The American Partnership.* Chicago: Chicago Univ. Press, 1962.

_____. *American Federalism: A View from the States.* New York: Thomas Y. Crowell, 1966.

Freeman, J. Leiper. *The Political Process: Executive Bureau-Legislative Committee Relations.* New York: Random House, 1955.

Graves, W. Brooke. *American Intergovernmental Relations.* New York: Scribner's, 1964.

Grodzins, Morton. *The American System,* Daniel T. Elazar (ed.). Chicago: Rand McNally, 1966.

Hawley, Willis D. *Where Governments Meet: Emerging Patterns of Intergovernmental Relations.* Berkeley, Calif.: Institute of Governmental Studies, Univ. of California, 1967.

Heller, Walter W. *New Dimensions of Political Economy.* Cambridge, Mass.: Harvard Univ. Press, 1966.

Jones, Charles O. *An Introduction to the Study of Public Policy.* Belmont, Calif.: Wadsworth Pub. Co., 1970.

Lindblom, Charles E. *The Intelligence of Democracy: Decision Making Through Mutual Adjustment.* New York: Free Press, 1965.

Macdonald, Austin F. *Federal Aid.* New York: Thomas Crowell, 1928.

Martin, Roscoe C. *The Cities and the Federal System.* New York: Atherton, 1965.

Maxwell, James A. *Financing State and Local Governments.* Washington: Brookings Institution, 1965.

Patterson, James T. *The New Deal and the States: Federalism in Transition.* Princeton, N.J.: Princeton Univ. Press, 1969.

Reagan, Michael D. *The New Federalism.* New York: Oxford Univ. Press, 1972.

Redford, Emmette S. *Democracy in the Administrative State.* New York: Oxford Univ. Press, 1969.

Reuss, Henry S. *Revenue Sharing: Crutch or Catalyst for State and Local Governments?* New York: Praeger, 1970.

Sanford, Terry. *Storm Over the States.* New York: McGraw-Hill, 1967.

Sharkansky, Ira (ed.). *Policy Analysis in Political Science.* Chicago: Markham Pub. Co., 1970.

Weidner, Edward W. *Intergovernmental Relations As Seen by Public Officials.* Minneapolis: Univ. of Minnesota Press, 1960.

ARTICLES AND OTHER PUBLICATIONS

Council of State Governments. *State Government.* Special Issue on Revenue Sharing. Winter 1973.

Dommel, Paul R. "Confusion Over Revenue Sharing," *The New Republic* (Nov. 30, 1968), pp. 12-13.

Frankel, Max. "Revenue Sharing Is a Counterrevolution," *The New York Times Magazine* (April 25, 1971), pp. 28ff.

Heller, Walter W. "Should the Government Share Its Tax Take?" *Saturday Review* (Mar. 22, 1969), pp. 26-29.

Jencks, Christopher. "Why Bail Out the States?" *The New Republic* (Dec. 12, 1964), pp. 8-10.

Joint Center for Political Studies. *The Minority Community and Revenue Sharing,* 2nd ed. Washington, D.C., June 1973.

Key, V.O. "Administration of Federal Grants to the States," *American Political Science Review.* March 1937.

Myers, Will S., Jr. "Fiscal Balance in the American Federal System," *State Government.* Winter 1968.

National Governors Conference. *Proceedings of the Thirty-Eighth Annual Meeting.* Chicago, 1946.

National League of Cities. "A First Look at City Use of Revenue Sharing Funds," *Nation's Cities.* Aug. 1973.

——————. "Revenue Sharing," *Nation's Cities.* April 1967.

National League of Cities/U.S. Conference of Mayors. *The Federal Budget and the Cities.* Washington, Feb. 1974.

"No More Depressions?" *U.S. News & World Report.* June 29, 1964.

Pechman, Joseph A. "Money for the States," *The New Republic.* April 8, 1967.

Notes

I. MAKING OF AN ISSUE

1. U. S., Congress, House of Representatives, Committee on Ways and Means, *Hearings, General Revenue Sharing, Part 1*, 92nd Cong., 1st Sess., June 1971, p. 41.

2. Charles O. Jones, *An Introduction to the Study of Public Policy* (Belmont Calif,: Wadsworth Pub. Co., 1970), pp. 27-32.

3. For a full discussion of the operations of the federal aid system in the 19th century, see Daniel J. Elazar, *The American Partnership* (Chicago: University of Chicago Press, 1962).

4. *The New York Times,* Nov. 28, 1971, p. 51.

5. L. L. Ecker-Racz, *The Politics and Economics of State-Local Finance* (Englewood Cliffs, N. J.: Prentice-Hall, 1970), p. 33.

6. U.S., Advisory Commission on Intergovernmental Relations, *The Role of Equalization in Federal Grants* (Washington: U.S. Government Printing Office, Jan. 1964).

7. *Fiscal Balance in the American Federal System, Vol. I* (Washington: U.S. Government Printing Office, Oct. 1967), pp. 139-45.

8. Ibid., p. 145.

9. U.S., Commission on Intergovernmental Relations, *An Advisory Committee Report on Local Government* (Washington: U.S. Government Printing Office, June 1955), p.1.

10. *Fiscal Balance,* p. 165.

11. *The Cities and the Federal System* (New York: Atherton Press, 1965).

12. *Storm Over the States* (New York: McGraw-Hill, 1967).

13. Ibid., p. 124.

14. Richard Blumenthal, "The Bureaucracy: Antipoverty and the Community Action Program," *American Political Institutions and Public Policy* (Boston: Little, Brown, 1969), pp. 128-79.

II. POLITICS OF POLICY INITIATIVE I

1. U.S., *Public Papers of the Presidents of the United States: Lyndon B. Johnson, 1963-64, Books I-II* (Washington: U.S. Government Printing Office, 1964), Book I, p. 113.

2. Ibid., p. 311.

3. "No More Depressions?" *U.S. News & World Report,* June 29, 1964, p. 59.

4. Arthur M. Schlesinger, Jr., *A Thousand Days: John F. Kennedy in the White House* (New York: Fawcett, 1967), pp. 148-54.

5. Norman C. Thomas and Harold L. Wolman, "Policy Formulation in the Institutionalized Presidency: The Johnson Task Forces," *The Presidential Advisory System,* ed. Thomas E. Cronin and Sanford D. Greenberg (New York: Harper & Row, 1969), pp. 124-28.

6. Interview with Joseph A. Pechman, Washington, D.C., Nov. 1971.

7. Walter W. Heller, *New Dimensions of Political Economy* (Cambridge: Harvard University Press, 1966), pp. 150-51.

8. Ibid., p. 166.

9. U.S., Congress, *Joint Hearings, Five-Year Record of the Advisory Commission on Intergovernmental Relations and Its Future Role,* Subcommittee on Intergovernmental Relations of the Senate and House Committee on Government Operations, 89th Cong., 1st Sess., 1965, p. 109.

10. *The New York Times,* Oct. 29, 1964, p. 19.

11. *Johnson Papers 1963-64, Book II,* p. 1462.

12. Ibid., p. 1485.

13. *The New York Times,* p. 14.

14. The House, by a vote of 224 to 201, reinstated the "twenty-one day rule" to prevent legislative delays in the Rules Committee. This permitted bringing legislation to the floor if the Rules Committee failed to grant a rule within twenty-one days. Such a procedure had been adopted by the 81st Congress in 1949, but it was deleted by the 82nd Congress in 1951. It was revived for just two years, again being dropped in 1967.

15. U.S., *Budget of the United States Government: 1966* (Washington: U.S. Government Printing Office, 1965), p. 17.

16. *U.S. Budget 1967,* p. 19.

17. *U.S. Budget 1968,* p. 7.

18. U.S., *Weekly Compilation of Presidential Documents,* II, No. 11 (Washington: U.S. Government Printing Office), p. 377.

19. Robert L. Heilbroner, "The Share-the-Tax Revenue Plan," *The New York Times Magazine,* Dec. 27, 1964, p. 31.

20. The questionnaire survey of member opinions on revenue sharing was made by the writer in the summer of 1967, asking whether, in general, Congressmen favored or opposed legislative proposals to return a fixed portion of federal income tax revenues to state and local governments. The results of this questionnaire became part of an unpublished Master's thesis, "Politics of Revenue Sharing and the Evolution of Grants-in-Aid," George Washington University, Washington, D.C., June 1968.

21. Only those roll call votes were tabulated on which there was an opposing vote of at least 15 percent of the votes cast. For those members new to Congress in 1967, the field was nine bills.

III. POLITICS OF POLICY INITIATIVE II

1. *U.S. Budget 1968*, p. 34.
2. Ibid.
3. U.S., *Economic Report of the President, 1967* (Washington: U.S. Government Printing Office, 1967), p. 24.
4. *Congressional Record*, Jan. 23, 1967 (Daily Edition), p. S652.
5. Ibid., Feb. 15, 1967 (Daily Edition), p. H1337.
6. U.S., *Public Papers of the Presidents of the United States: Lyndon B. Johnson, 1967, Books I-II* (Washington: U.S. Government Printing Office, 1968), Book I, pp. 134-45.
7. Ibid., pp. 331-46.
8. Ibid., p. 366. The quote which follows is from p. 367.
9. *Congressional Record*, Jan. 30, 1967 (Daily Edition), p. H776.
10. See Stephen K. Bailey, *The Office of Education and the Education Act of 1965*, Inter-University Case Program #100 (New York: Bobbs-Merrill, 1966).
11. *The New York Times*, Feb. 7, 1967, p. 1.
12. U.S., Congress, Subcommittee on Fiscal Policy of the Joint Economic Committee, *Hearings, Revenue-Sharing and Its Alternatives: What Future for Fiscal Federalism?*, 90th Cong., 1st Sess., 1967.
13. *The Washington Post*, Oct. 10, 1967, p. 9.
14. *The New York Times*, Nov. 20, 1966, p. 39.
15. Ibid., Oct. 27, 1968, Financial Section, p. 14.

IV. BUILDING A COALITION

1. From "Summary of Report of Intergovernmental Fiscal Relations Task Force." The summary, prepared by Richard P. Nathan, was dated

April 11, 1969. Interview with Nathan, Washington, D.C., November 1971.

2. *The New York Times,* Jan. 15, 1969, p. 1.

3. *The New York Times,* Dec. 15, 1968, p. 1.

4. *Congressional Record,* Jan. 15, 1969 (Daily Edition), p. S298.

5. From table: *Congressional Record,* March 20, 1969 (Daily Edition), pp. S3004-05.

6. *The New York Times,* Feb. 10, 1967, p. 22.

7. S. 2483, June 25, 1969.

8. S. 1634, March 24, 1969.

9. In June 1969, the U. S. Conference of Mayors adopted a resolution urging Congress to amend the program because of the way funds were being distributed. Ten days later a meeting of midwest governors praised the way the program was operated. For full discussion of the issue, see: U.S., Congress, Senate, *Federal Assistance to Law Enforcement,* Hearings before the Subcommittee on Criminal Laws and Procedures of the Committee on the Judiciary, 91st. Congress, 2nd Sess., June 24, 25, July 7 and 30, 1970.

10. Text of Nixon message, *The New York Times,* Aug. 14, 1969, p. 24.

11. Ibid.

12. Identical bills subsequently introduced were H.R. 14021, 14044, 14327, 19740.

13. S. 2948, Sept. 23, 1969.

14. Dom Bonafede, "Revenue Sharing Report/The Nixon Plan's Premise: America's Federal System Is Not Working," *National Journal,* April 3, 1971, pp. 704-05.

15. *The New York Times,* Dec. 2, 1970, p. 1.

V. NEW PLAN; NEW CONTROVERSIES

1. *The New York Times,* Jan. 6, 1971, p. 1.

2. Ibid., Jan. 21, 1971, p. 1.

3. Ibid., Aug. 14, 1969, p. 1; and Jan. 23, 1971, p. 1.

4. U.S., Congress, Senate, Subcommittee on Intergovernmental Relations of the Committee on Government Operations, *Hearings, Intergovernmental Revenue Act of 1971 and Related Legislation,* 92nd Cong., 1st Sess., June and Aug. 1971, p. 85.

5. Information on the formulation process came from author's interviews and material in the files of Edwin Harper, Domestic Council, The White House, Nov. 1971; letters from Murray Weidenbaum, former Assistant Secretary of the Treasury, to the author.

6. The specifics come from the sources in the preceding note.

7. *The New York Times,* Jan. 26, 1971, p. 1.

8. *Congressional Record,* Jan. 26, 1971 (Daily Edition), pp. H210-15.

9. Dom Bonafede, "Revenue Sharing Report/The Nixon Plan's Premise: America's Federal System Is Not Working," *National Journal,* April 3, 1971, pp. 705-06.

VI. CONGRESS ENACTS A LAW

1. U.S., House of Representatives, *Hearings, General Revenue Sharing,* Parts 1-8, Committee on Ways and Means, 92nd Cong., 1st Sess., 1971.

2. Ibid., p. 37.

3. Ibid., p. 48.

4. Ibid., p. 217-218.

5. Ibid., p. 219.

6. Ibid., p. 493.

7. Ibid.

8. Ibid., p. 713.

9. Ibid., p. 453.

10. Ibid., p. 454.

11. Ibid., pp. 1307-08.

12. *The New York Times,* May 11, 1971, p. 23.

13. *Hearings,* p. 51.

14. *The New York Times,* June 11, 1971, pp. 1, 14.

15. *Hearings,* p. 804.

16. For an expanded study of the Joint Committee on Internal Revenue Taxation, see: John Manley, "Congressional Staff and Public Policy-Making: The Joint Committee on Internal Revenue Taxation," *The Journal of Politics,* Vol. 30, No. 4, Nov. 1968, pp. 1046-47.

17. *The New York Times,* July 4, 1971, p. 24.

18. Ibid., July 23, 1971, p. 13.

19. Ibid., July 22, 1971, p. 1.

20. Ibid., Feb. 16, 1972, p. 20.

21. Ibid., Mar. 7, 1972, p. 27.

22. U.S., House of Representatives, Committee on Ways and Means, *State and Local Fiscal Assistance Act of 1972,* 92nd Cong., 2d Sess., April 26, 1972, H. Rept. 1018, Part I, to accompany H.R. 14370.

23. Data from: Americans for Constitutional Action, *ACA Index: An Analysis of the Voting Record of Each Member in the Congress of the United States,* 1st Sess., 92d Cong., 1971, Washington, D.C.; Americans for

Democratic Action, *ADA World*, Jan., Nov.-Dec. 1972, Washington, D.C.

24. *Congressional Record*, June 22, 1972 (Daily Edition), p. H5949.

25. U.S., Senate, Committee on Finance, *Revenue Sharing Act of 1972*, 92d Cong., 2d Sess., Aug. 16, 1972, S. Rept. 1050, Part I, to accompany H.R. 14370, p. 22.

26. Ibid., pp. 65-66.

27. U.S., Senate, Committee on Conference, *State and Local Fiscal Assistance Act of 1972*, 92d Cong., 2d Sess., Sept. 26, 1972, S. Rept. 1229, to accompany H.R. 14370.

28. U.S., *Weekly Compilation of Presidential Documents*, VIII, No. 43 (Washington: U.S. Government Printing Office, 1972), pp. 1534, 1535.

VII. IMPLEMENTATION: PROBLEMS AND ISSUES

1. *The New York Times*, Nov. 10, 1972, p. 20.

2. Ibid., Nov. 28, 1972, p. 27.

3. Ibid., Dec. 1, 1972, p. 22.

4. U.S., *Budget of the United States Government: 1974* (Washington: U.S. Government Printing Office, 1973), p. 16.

5. Ibid., p. 122.

6. U.S., Congress, Senate, Subcommittee on Intergovernmental Relations of the Committee on Government Operations, *Hearings, A New Federalism*, 93rd Cong., 1st Sess., Feb. and Mar., 1973.

7. *U.S. Budget 1975*.

8. National League of Cities/U.S. Conference of Mayors, *The Federal Budget and the Cities* (Washington, Feb. 1974), p. 5.

9. Brochure: U.S. Department of the Treasury, Office of Revenue Sharing, *General Revenue Sharing: Allocations and Adjustments* (Washington: U.S. Government Printing Office, 1973).

10. U.S., Department of the Treasury, Office of Revenue Sharing, *Preliminary Survey of General Revenue Sharing Recipient Governments*, an unpublished report made by Technology Management Inc., June 19, 1973. The percentages which follow come from page 10.

11. U.S., Comptroller General of the United States, *Revenue Sharing: Its Use by and Impact on State Governments* (Washington, Aug. 2, 1973), pp. 1-2.

12. U.S., Department of the Treasury, Office of Revenue Sharing, *General Revenue Sharing: The First Actual Use Reports* (Washington: U.S. Government Printing Office, Mar. 1974).

13. Ibid., p. 43.
14. Ibid., p. 16.
15. *Preliminary Survey* (TMI), p. 8.
16. Ibid., p. 9.

Index